STOPPING RAPE

# STOPPING RAPE
## *A Challenge for Men*

*by*

RUS ERVIN FUNK

NEW SOCIETY PUBLISHERS

*Philadelphia, PA*     *Gabriola Island, BC*

Inquiries regarding requests to reprint all or part of *Stopping Rape: A Challenge for Men* should be addressed to:
New Society Publishers
4527 Springfield Avenue
Philadelphia, PA 19143

ISBN USA 0-86571-267-0 Hardcover
ISBN USA 0-86571-268-9 Paperback
ISBN CAN 1-55092-210-6 Hardcover
ISBN CAN 1-55092-211-4 Paperback

Printed in the United States of America on partially recycled paper using soy ink by Capital City Press of Montpelier, Vermont.

Cover by Brian Prendergast.
Backcover photograph by Bill Christensen.
Book design by Martin Kelley.

To order directly from the publisher, add $2.50 to the price for the first copy, 75¢ to the price for each additional copy. Send check or money order to:
New Society Publishers
4527 Springfield Avenue
Philadelphia, PA 19143
In Canada, contact:
New Society Publishers/New Catalyst
PO Box 189
Gabriola Island, BC V0R 1X0

New Society Publishers is a project of the New Society Educational Foundation, a nonprofit, tax-exempt, public foundation in the United States, and of the Catalyst Education Society, a nonprofit society in Canada. Opinions expressed in this book do not necessarily represent positions of the New Society Educational Foundation, nor the Catalyst Education Society.

This book is dedicated to my parents, Betty and Merle Funk,
the National Coalition Against Sexual Assault,
the members of DC Men Against Rape,
and to a world free of rape.

"The most radical step you can take is your next one."
—James Baldwin

# CONTENTS

# PREFACE

WRITING THIS BOOK has been an incredible experience. I wish I could describe fully what it's been like—it's been exciting, fulfilling, thrilling, scary—made more so because 1993 marks my tenth anniversary of being involved in the struggle to end rape. There's a part of this experience that seems very fitting in that light.

However, by and large, writing this book has been excruciating. It would have been much easier if I could have intellectualized about rape for the past nine months and written this from my brain instead of from my heart and soul. But I can't—not and be fair to you, the survivors, the issues, and myself. For months on end, I've been thinking and feeling about rape. For weeks at a time, rape has been the last thing on my mind before falling asleep, and the first thing I think about when I get up. I've been thinking about, talking about, dreaming about, feeling about, reading about, considering, theorizing, and trying to write about rape; and translating all these experiences and information in a manner that you can understand.

I've been a real bummer at parties and dinners—talking with friends about these issues and trying to come up with a way to talk about rape that is clearer and easier to understand (not exactly a fun dinner topic). I've gone to movies with friends—and left in the middle to write a paragraph in my seemingly ever-present notebook. I've gotten short-tempered from time to time because I stayed up too late trying to finish that last paragraph—and then didn't sleep well for the nightmares and tension that I carried to bed with me. I've been moody, at times despondent, and often have felt just plain raw! There have been times when, sitting on the subway, I've begun to cry for no apparent reason, times when I've laughed inappropriately, and times when I've flown into a rage. I feel very similar to the way I felt when I first began doing this work and hadn't yet learned how not to get caught up in the intensity and pain survivors feel. Since then, I've learned to do that, but learning to write a book requires a new set of skills—skills I haven't developed yet.

However, I also know that despite how raw I feel right now, and the depth of emotions I'm swimming in, what I feel in no way compares to the feelings of survivors of sexual violence. It is for you that I write this book. It is to you that I am most accountable. And for the day that we can truthfully say that there will be no more—no more rape.

I'm very much looking forward to getting back to doing the work that I've tried to describe here. Being tied to my computer for days on end has left me feeling very alone in this morass of emotions that I still don't know what I'm going to do with. I'm looking forward to meeting people again, and organizing, planning and acting up again. But more than anything else, I look forward to a day when the need for this book will be obsolete.

— Rus Ervin Funk,
Washington, DC

# ACKNOWLEDGMENTS

THERE ARE A large number of people who have been a part of this process—too many for me to name here. But a few deserve special attention. Writing this book has been an incredible experience—not all of it good. Many of you have been there throughout this process, and I know that I haven't reciprocated the support and incredible patience you've shown. I appreciate it more than you can know. I hesitate writing out any names for fear of forgetting someone who deserves special mention.

First off, there are a number of women who were the first to show me these connections and who were there when I started down this journey ten years ago. I need to thank those women, who were among the first to confront, educate, and sensitize me about men's violence and the possibilities to end men's violence. Among these truly incredible women are Cindy Medina, Delma Gomez, Elva Enriquéz, Linda Webster, Debby Tucker, Cassandra Thomas, Lacey Sloan, and Sherry Abbott. Each of you have had a major impact on my early development. You were the sisters who were present during those first few years that in many ways were the most intense. You watched me struggle—and generally let me struggle—for it was my struggle to have. I love you all, and appreciate you more than you can know!

More recently, a number of women have continued where these women left off. Nikki Craft, Phoenix, and Phyllis Chesler, you have been tireless in your support and encouragement—although at times I've wondered why. You have also been the most up front in challenging me when I've needed it. Maggie Clark is among my longest-running friends and has seen me through some serious trials and tribulations. You've always been there with a hug and a willingness to be honest—even when

I haven't wanted to hear what you've had to say. Cris South and Roxanne Seagraves (as well as Gavin, Mitzie, and Pogo) have always provided me with a warm, sane place to stay when my life gets too crazy (which is frequently) as well as calming thoughts; Kathryn Naylor, dance partner and soul mate—my relationship with you has always defied description; Laura Navarro, Valarie Sperling, and Chris Warden, you have been truly amazing in your support and friendship! You have all come into my life and been amazing sources of encouragement, inspiration, and stability. The friendship you have shown me has been a true gift. I've been blessed!

I also want to thank Jack Straton and Gerry Sutter, who cofounded the first Men Against Rape group that I came into contact with and who drew me seriously into the anti-sexist men's movement. Both Jack and Gerry have continued to be strong friends, and constant supporters—I love you both.

Martin DeFresne, Vernon McClean, Craig Norberg-Bohm, Elias Farajaja-Jones—I don't think I could have done this without your support, your encouragement, and just knowing that you've been there. Further, all of you have a clarity that is amazing, and each of you has furthered my thinking in ways I simply can not describe.

The men of DC Men Against Rape over the past six years: Mike Airhart, Bill Christensen, Max Freund, David Kirchner, Patrick Lemmon, Jonathan Stillerman, Jim Watts, Steve Wendell, Tom Wilde (I know I've left some of you out): You have been there throughout my development and my growth. *You* are who this book is for and about. Thank you . . . and here's to many more years of good work together.

Jon Cohen, Darryl Spears, Jeffry Basen-Engquist, and John Stoltenberg—I don't know what to say. Whenever I've called, written, or been in contact there has always been a hug, a smile, and *lots* to think (and rethink) about. You, as much as any other, have made this book what it is. I'm glad you are in my life!

My housemates—Mary Melchior and Sean Mahaffey, have been through this process almost alongside me. You've put up with my moodiness, and endless hours I've been at the computer—late into the night and first thing in the morning. I *deeply* appreciate your supporting me and putting up with me.

Martin Kelley and the staff of New Society have been amazing to work with. My clarity hasn't always been on the surface, but you've always found it and pulled it out of me. I have rarely found a business run with more integrity and sincerity than NSP. I'm a better person for having worked with you.

Margo Adair has helped in quiet and strong ways. You've helped me strengthen my words and my vision. And you've forced me to be precise and clear. Thank you.

Sam Diener has been a constant voice of reason in terms of my writing—and my life. You have helped more than any other in bringing this book to light. Sam, who is also a longtime soulmate and Frisbee partner: my love for you just continues to grow. When I've gotten too arrogant, you've helped me see it; and when I got too down on myself for whatever reason, you helped pull me through. Thanks for being in such a profound space in my life!

Finally, two people who have made all this possible: my parents, Betty and Merle Funk. You gave me the strength to be who I am and do what I need to do. You provided me with the foundation I needed to be in the world as fully empowered and liberated as I've become. And despite our disagreements, you have always loved and supported me even when you haven't been able to support my choices. More than my parents, you are my friends, and I love you!

# INTRODUCTION

MEN ARE TRYING to find new ways to coexist with women. As men, we are struggling with what it means to "be a man" in the nineties. The growing numbers of men's organizations, men's publications, and men's activities examining what it means to "be a man" and attempting to redefine masculinity are evidence of this confusion. Because of challenges from women, men (and most certainly women) know that the old ways of interrelating (man-to-man, and man-to-woman) no longer work (if they ever did). Men aren't happy and plainly aren't healthy: We hurt and kill women, children, and each other; we die younger than women; we suffer from loneliness, isolation, depression, and general unhappiness; we have higher rates of suicide and addiction than women; we spend a much greater proportion of our lives in prison than women. The list continues, and continues to grow.

Finally, over the past fifteen or so years, men have begun talking with each other, developing "men's consciousness-raising groups," creating a "mytho-poetic" men's movement and establishing a men's anti-sexist movement. All of these developments indicate that men are grappling with the issues of what we have been taught about "being a man." Men seem to be realizing that trying to live up to the old "John Wayne" and "Rambo" myths of manhood isn't enough and isn't satisfactory, yet we don't seem to know what needs to change or how to change.

Much of this reexamination is indebted to the work of feminists. The U.S. feminist movement of the early sixties and seventies was marked by consciousness raising or "CR" groups—women coming together to discuss what it means to "be a woman." Out of these discussions came a growing political awareness that many of the difficulties that women face are not due to individual failings as they had been led to believe but are instead caused by sexism and living in a male-dominated society. Coupled with

1

the sisterly solidarity engendered by CR groups, this growing awareness has fueled powerful and dynamic feminist movements in the United States and around the world. As a result of the questions that women began asking, men have begun to reexamine what our roles are, what our relationship to women and to each other may be, and how those relationships may have changed, are changing, or must change.

As an outgrowth of these CR groups, women redefined rape as a social problem deserving a direct, compassionate, and effective societal response. Women began identifying ways to support themselves and each other, as well as how to support other women victimized by men. In the early days, women used their personal phones as hot lines, and made time in their schedules to listen supportively, and accompany other women to the hospital as well as through the often brutal process of reporting and healing from sexual violence. The first rape crisis centers were established in this country in the early 1970s. From these grew the current network of rape crisis centers, battered women's shelters, and anti-pornography educating and activism. Currently several large national feminist networks are working on these issues.

Out of this new political awareness also grew an understanding of how men's violence is overwhelmingly and overpoweringly directed at women and children. Part of the discussion which follows will reexamine the levels of men's violence and the awareness that women created from those early CR groups. The purpose of this reexamination is neither to blame nor to "guilt" men. Rather, my purpose is to define men's violence and to re-expose the extent of our violence. The only way to begin working towards solutions is to come to a clear understanding of the parameters of the problem. It is vital for men's voices to begin labeling and defining men's violence and breaking the silence(s) surrounding our violence. Women have been doing just that for centuries. Now, men must start listening to women, and raising our own voices against our violence, for breaking the silences around our violence is the beginning of putting an end to men's violence.

Rape is traditionally defined as a "women's problem." Part of this idea is based on the fact that women are the overwhelming majority—*70 percent*—of the victims and survivors of men's sexual violence (Russell, 1984, p.77). Additionally, women were the first to publicly define the need and begin the work to ensure that women, children, and men who are raped have somewhere to turn. Third, feminists reinterpreted rape as the political issue that it is. Women were the first and are still in the forefront pushing society to perceive rape as both a personal trauma and a political crime (See Connell and Wilson, *Rape: The First Sourcebook for Women*, 1974).

Tragically, given this cultural misdefinition, rape has been relegated into the arena of other so-called women's issues. Thus rape, like so many other "women's problems," is defined as a personal mental health issue that must be addressed in therapy or in some other arena—behind closed doors. Rape, like other "women's issues," is trivialized, thrown in with other sociopolitical issues like cooking, sewing, childcare, etc. The common assumption is that women ought to deal with and solve these issues privately; they aren't perceived important enough to be dealt with on a public policy or community level.

Contrary to this misinformation, rape is a men's issue. Rape says much more about men than it ever has about women. Rape is a louder statement about masculinity than it is about femininity. Consider—what does it say about women that nearly one in two will be sexually victimized? And what does it say about men that many of us are sexually victimizing—and the rest of us have nothing to say about the issue? I suggest that it says a lot about us in terms of "being a man"—a lot that we may not be particularly comfortable in examining—but which we must!

Most men would agree that rape is one of the most traumatic and painful experiences that anyone—male or female—could go through. Few, however, devote as much concern and energy to this issue as to chemical addictions, for example. The chemical addictions movement has gotten a great deal of male and societal support and ongoing encouragement. One need only look at the amount of energy, time, and money that is spent to "keep kids clean" or the number of programs available for addicts (which, agreed, is not enough) to see the ways that, socially and politically, we have begun to respond to issues of chemical dependency.

Rape however has received virtually no societal nor male response. The physical and mental damage from rape and incest is often as devastating, if not more so, than the damage caused by addictions, and a similar, if not greater, number of people are affected by men's sexual violence as are affected by addictions. Yet men's sexual violence elicits neither the recognition, support, nor moral outrage (except on the part of rape survivors and sometimes their significant others) that other issues like addictions receive. It is essential that we as men and we as a society begin responding appropriately and proactively to issues of sexual violence. Not only must we respond to the women and men in our lives who have been victimized, but we need to respond in a broader way to the issue as a whole. We, as men, must begin taking response-ability for rape and for the sociocultural climate that encourages rape. We, as men, must begin working towards a world where there is no more rape.

Men have been called upon for years to answer the cries of women and children. These cries too often fall silently into the night. This book, which is breaking new ground as the first book against rape specifically for men, is about breaking ground, and breaking the silence. It is about listening to women and children, and about what we will hear.

This book is written by a man, for men, about men; and is focused on the ways men can work to end men's violence. Most men claim to be opposed to violence, and against rape and battery. Unfortunately, the movements to end men's violence are still overwhelmingly female, and the pro-feminist men's movement continues to be plagued with painfully low membership and a general lack of effectiveness.

This book is for men who may or may not have ever acted abusively against women, but who are interested in working to end men's violence; and for women who want to know what men can do, or how to work with men. It is not enough to be "another man against men's violence" (a Donnelly-Colt button slogan); not enough for us to oppose rape; not enough for us to participate in Take Back the Night marches or donate money to local battered women's shelters or rape crisis centers. It is not enough for us to learn to talk with each other or to cry, or to learn how to carry a baby, change a diaper, or interact lovingly with children. All of these activities are essential and necessary and important and wonderful. But none of this is enough—all of this is not enough. Doing all of these things will not stop men's violence. Men's violence begins and will end with the "man in the mirror," and with our willingness to confront ourselves, each other, and our society until men don't rape anymore. This book is about that self-examination and why this self-examination, painful and difficult as it is, is so critical. Men are more than strong enough and creative enough to muddle our different ways through. This book is about love, hope, and a deep faith in our ability to change.

I deeply believe that we are more than our past and current behaviors demonstrate. We can all be so very much more. Rarely have men made the opportunity to develop a deep and honest appreciation of the profound impact that rape has on the lives of women and men. Men who are becoming sensitized have an obligation to become further educated and pass on this training and information to others. The only way to begin taking steps towards that end is to begin taking steps, and begin examining where we currently are. That kind of self-scrutiny will indeed make us uncomfortable. It is up to you what you do with these feelings of discomfort. I only hope that you choose to move, for move we must!

It is my hope that this book will become a tool of liberation—for men as well as for women, and for children. The words held within these pages may indeed make you uncomfortable or make you squirm. In fact, that's my desire, for no movement happens, no revolutions occur without some discomfort, without some shaking of our safety. As Frederick Douglass said,

> For those who profess to favor freedom, and yet depreciate agitation, are those who want crops without plowing up the ground. They want rain without thunder and lightening. They want the ocean without the awful roar of its waters. This struggle may be a moral one; or it may be a physical one; or it may be both moral and physical; but it must be a struggle. (letter to an abolitionist friend, 1849)

We live in a world where men's sexual violence is so commonplace as to be considered all but natural. Few people consider a world where rape isn't a reality. Can you imagine? Can you picture a world where women aren't threatened by every man, and every man is not a threat? Can you imagine how we, as men and women, adults and children, would interact if the threat of rape were removed? I urge you to try. Try to picture just such a world, a world where, as John Stoltenberg describes it, "gender justice" reigns.

I hope to encourage men to begin seriously and effectively discussing the issue of sexual violence; most important, how men benefit and how to stop all forms of rape. I have three main purposes: to increase men's awareness and sensitivity around men's sexual violence, to increase men's skills and willingness to confront rape behavior and sexism, and to develop the aptitude and comfort necessary to talk with other men about these issues. We don't all necessarily need to become public speakers to begin confronting rape. Whenever and wherever men congregate, we, as men, have the opportunity to discuss, confront, and eliminate rape-supporting attitudes, beliefs, and behaviors. Men can stop rape!

# ONE

# RAPE
## *The Personal Tragedy*

THIS SECTION IS an attempt to offer an honest description of rape: the realities and the experiences of rape survivors. As such, it is graphic. My attempt is not to shock you, but it is important that we all become more sensitized to the trauma and the impacts of rape on people's lives. Do what you need to do in order to take care of yourself while reading this section, but also allow yourself to *feel* the impact reading this has on you and compare that to the experience being raped has on survivors.

The number of women victimized by men's violence is staggering: 42 percent of women survive completed or attempted sexual assault in their lifetimes (Russell 1984, p.35), 54 percent of women are battered by their male partners (National Coalition Against Domestic Violence 1990), 78 percent of women are sexually harassed by men in their workplace or their classroom (MacKinnon, Paludi), and one in five men are sexually abused by the time they are eighteen (Lew—this is the only solid statistic currently available on the incidence of male sexual assault).

Rape is also on the increase. For the past ten years, according to the United States Department of Justice Bureau of Justice Statistics, rape has been the *only* crime that has continuously increased, and has been the fastest growing violent crime in the country (increasing by a whopping *48 percent* in 1991 alone). Possibly this increase is a result of the feminist rape crisis movement and its efforts to increase the responsiveness of the legal system, but the sheer magnitude of survivors and therefore perpetrators that these numbers represent is staggering.

In addition, we are currently seeing dramatic increases in racist, religion-based, and homophobic hate violence, which is overwhelmingly perpetrated by men. These hate crimes put women at increased risk on

7

two levels. First of all, women of color, Jewish and Muslim women, and lesbians and bisexual women are doubly at risk for surviving a violent hate crime. Secondly, because of the factors in hate violence, often a sexual assault component occurs as well. Rarely do women, even women who are extremely bigoted, act out their hatred in violent ways.

These statistics aren't just numbers—as terrifying as they are on that level alone. We know these people. These are the human beings in our lives. Sexual assault is a horribly traumatic crime that affects real people to the very core of who they are and who they believe themselves to be. Given these statistics, it is extremely likely that we know these women and men—they are in our lives, in our homes, in our workplaces, in our neighborhoods, in our classes. They are our colleagues, our housemates, our sisters, and our lovers. We very probably know rape survivors very intimately, although we don't know that they are survivors. "Coming out" about being a survivor is rather similar to "coming out" about being gay or bisexual: It's dangerous, it's scary, and it requires incredible bravery. One of the best ways for us as men to start working against sexual assault is to assume that we know women and men who have been victimized—assume that rape has already come into our lives. Believe that it's already had an impact on you—albeit indirectly, but an impact nonetheless. Once you become someone survivors feel comfortable talking to about their experiences, they will. Assume it, and prepare for it.

### What Is Rape? Definitions and Effects

The definitions I offer below are a place to start. They aren't definitive. These definitions are meant to give us a common language from which to begin discussing issues of rape and sexual violence—something that we, as men, haven't had.

*Victim:* Women, children, or men who have died during the rape attack.

*Survivor:* Those who have physically survived rape attack(s).

*Sexuality:* Who we are and how we define ourselves as sexual beings. This individual interpretation includes how we define ourselves as "male" or "female," how we define our sexual orientation, as well as how we choose to express those definitions (i.e., how we like to share sexually, with whom we like to share sexually, etc.).

*Rape:* Forced contact or penetration of the anus, vagina, or mouth by any object or body part. Rape is usually categorized in three main ways: stranger rape, acquaintance rape (including friends, co-workers, customers, classmates, dates, etc.), and marital rape. Gang rape occurs in all of these instances.

*Sexual Assault:* Any forced or unwanted sexual contact as *defined by the victim/survivor.*

*Sexual Harassment:* Referring to women or men as sexual beings in inappropriate environments, such as the workplace, classroom, or on the streets; or in demeaning, intimidating, or threatening ways, such as whistling, catcalling, or touching. Or behaving in ways that result in a hostile or intimidating environment. Again, it is the survivor who defines what is and what isn't appropriate behavior.

*Gender Harassment:* Not allowing women to forget that they are women—thereby effectively reinforcing the idea that women are somehow "out of place" or don't belong and aren't capable because of their gender.

*Incest:* The sexual victimization or exploitation of a child by a family member or pseudo-family member (i.e., mother's boyfriend).

*Child Sexual Abuse:* The sexual victimization or exploitation of a child by an adult other than a family member.

## THE PERSONAL TRAUMA OF RAPE

Rape is traumatic on a number of levels. On the physical level, rape is forcing a body to do what the body may not want to do nor be prepared to do. When people are raped, they are forced to be sexual, without being ready or prepared. As such, their vaginal or anal muscles are tensed; with no lubrication, the walls surrounding these muscles are dry and as a result their bodies are being, sometimes literally, ripped open. Additionally, because of the emotional, physical, and spiritual levels of trauma, their bodies are tensed and are fighting against the forced intrusion. These muscles are consequently forced open, pulled apart, or torn into. The parts of the body being attacked during a rape are very sensitive parts: breasts, vagina, mouth, anus. These parts are hit, scratched, bitten, held down, pulled, forced open, prodded, poked:

> He grabbed me from behind. He threw me down and I knew, instinctively, what he was going to do. He kept tearing at my clothes, ripping them off. I fought back, but couldn't get him to stop. He was so much stronger. I kept trying to scream . . . and would open my mouth, but no sounds would come out. I was so terrified. He didn't have a knife or anything, but he could kill me. I couldn't breathe.

> I was dry and it felt like he was rubbing me with sandpaper. Every thrust seemed to take forever, and felt like a hot knife poking into my raw vagina. I kept hearing tearing—and thought it was clothing. Only later did I realize it was me that was tearing. As a result of the attack, he ripped away part of my outer labia majora, my clitoris is permanently damaged, I have scar tissue all through my vagina which has lessened my sensitivity to sex. (Anonymous)

Alongside the physical level, rape is also emotionally traumatic. Rape survivors lose control of a very special and intimate part of their lives—a part that in a very unique and special way is theirs and theirs alone. This is true not only on the physical level, but on the emotional and spiritual levels as well. Who we are sexually, and how we define ourselves as sexual beings, is at the very center of how we define ourselves as human beings: as male or female; how we express ourselves as "men," "women," or androgynes; as heterosexual, homosexual, bisexual, or celibate; and the ways that we like to share sexually. If we can control nothing more about who we are and how we express ourselves, we can control ourselves as sexual beings. We can decide who we share sex with and how we share sex. We can define how we express ourselves sexually. We can create what we individually and personally define as our own sexuality. We can choose how much of our sexual selves we want to express. For example, there are times when all of us put the sexual parts of ourselves very "out there" and other times when we are more demure about our sexuality. This is not to say or imply in any way that all of our sexuality is a choice. But how we express our sexuality certainly is. And more than anything else about who we are, how, when, and with whom we express our sexuality is a personal and intimate decision. Having control over this part of ourselves is at the base of all our beliefs of personal rights, individual autonomy, and bodily integrity. Without control of our sexual selves, none of those ideals can mean anything.

When a person survives a sexual assault, she or he experiences another person attacking this very intimate part of who we are—often in a physically violent way. As a result, everything we believe about the inherent rights of personal autonomy and bodily integrity are utterly destroyed. Unfortunately, we don't, as yet, have the language to adequately describe the experience nor the impact. These ideas and beliefs are directly attacked. This, in part, is what feminists are referring to when they define rape as an act of violence.

On another level, we express who we are as sexual beings in all aspects of our everyday behavior. Much of how we express ourselves as human beings reflects an expression of ourselves as sexual beings: the way we dress, walk, talk, and drive, ad infinitum, are all, in some ways, expressions of our sexual selves. When someone attacks that part of ourselves, it becomes difficult to do much of anything that does not, in some way, remind people of the attack they survived, and the part of themselves that was attacked.

All of us have certain feelings about our sexuality: our genital areas, our breasts, and our bodies in general. We all have ways that we like to share sexually; parts of our bodies that we particularly like; ways that we like to be touched; notions of what "good sex" is and isn't. This is the part of the person that is being attacked with rape:

> After the attack, I couldn't even stand to have my father touch me. I didn't even like to be real close to him. I just didn't want any bodily contact at all.
> —"Paula" (from Robin Warshaw, *I Never Called it Rape*)

> I became celibate for 8 years after the rape. I didn't want to touch, didn't want to be touched. I still am not sure about being sexual.
> —"John," raped by a stranger

> I wanted to lose my femininity, any sense of vulnerability. I became asexual—not just in that I didn't have sex, but in how I expressed myself. I never realized before how sexual we are. But after the rape, I went to extraordinary lengths to not be a sexual person. I cut my hair short, I refused to wear makeup, I wore only baggy clothes, I refused to notice people who were attractive.... In a lot of ways, I really stopped living.
> —"Tawana," raped by a classmate

When women or men are assaulted by acquaintances (which accounts for upwards of 90 percent of all sexual violence), not only are they left to experience and move through the emotions described above, but the attack challenges their belief in their ability to choose people to trust:

> I'm not sure if you can understand this, but I trusted him. I knew him and I let him into my home. I liked him . . . and he raped me. There were no warning signs, no bad behaviors, no indications of any kind that he would ever do anything like this. And yet he did. How am I ever going to be able to trust myself again. How am I supposed to know who I can trust and who I can't—since my instincts are obviously so off. How?
> —"Rachael," raped by a date

They agreed to go out with him or to let him into their home. They *wanted* to share with him and apparently liked him on some level. They may have acted on that attraction in terms of sharing kissing, hugging, or making out. They trusted their instincts that he really did "just want to study" or to work on the project. They believed that he was truthful in coming over to fix the furnace or the telephone. Their instincts led them to believe that this man was safe and would do them no harm. As such they often *feel* some complicity in the rape. Not only were they betrayed by the man, but they also *feel* betrayed by their own skills at keeping them safe from danger. It's essential to distinguish between feelings and truth. The feeling is real and valid and should be listened to . . . but it is not true! Survivors do not betray themselves; their instincts are fine. The man who rapes betrays them. He shoulders complete and sole responsibility for the hurt he caused. This is not to say that survivors are powerless, or that there aren't things that we can do to lessen our chances of being victimized. But when someone is raped, they are not complicit in the betrayal.

When women or men are attacked by strangers, a rape can exaggerate the fear that most women feel of male strangers, the outside, darkness, crowds, etc. Survivors of stranger rape often report that they never quite feel safe outside their own home. They describe what it's like to walk down the street not knowing which men are the potential threats, and which are relatively safe. They discuss the need to keep their guard up at *all* times, because of the attack(s) they survived. These feelings are not unknown to most women. Most women don't feel safe at night, or walking alone. Most women have some fear around strange men and describe the ways that they feel guarded when away from home. For survivors these feelings are intensified.

The feelings are often compounded by the specifics of the attack—where the attack occurred, at what time of day or night, whether weapons were used and how, whether there was more than one attacker, and whether the attacker was someone that the victim/survivor knew. All of these have an impact on the rest of the life of the person who has survived a sexual attack:

> I can't go out at night anymore. Every time I do, I'm afraid. I'm committed to not living my life afraid, and to trying to live as completely as I can—but *I'm always afraid!*
>
> I was attacked by 4 white men. Every time I see more than 2 white men together, I have to cross the street, get away, go the other direction.
>
> —"Cherrie"

When lesbians, gay men, and bisexuals are sexually victimized by heterosexuals (often during gay-bashing attacks), they often experience increased feelings of fear around being "out" and living their lifestyle in an open manner. When gay or bisexual men are sexually assaulted by gay or bi men, the survivor may feel incredibly conflicted. As one survivor put it:

> It isn't safe in the world because of heterosexism and violence perpetrated against me for being gay. It isn't safe for me to date men because they might rape me. What the hell am I supposed to do?!?
> —"Fred"

Gay men, bisexuals, and lesbians are left with a double whammy. Not only are they forced to recover from the sexual assault, they are forced to do so in a context in which their lifestyle is condemned and violence against them condoned by the dominant culture. The result is an increase in self-hate due to the self-blame most survivors experience, coupled with the internalized heterosexism that teaches us all to hate the homosexual parts of ourselves.

Additionally, these survivors often have difficulty receiving an appropriate response from services: the legal system (to which they often can not be "out"), crisis centers that are set up to assume the heterosexuality of the survivors, programs working with gay or bisexual survivors of violence that often aren't prepared to respond to victims of sexual violence, particularly when perpetrated by gays or bisexuals. And a court system that, in many states, still puts people in jail for acting out their gay lifestyle. Further, there still aren't adequate services available for gay survivors of sexual violence, especially acquaintance rape, within the gay community.

When people of color are attacked, a sexual assault can often reinforce the racism of our culture. When people of a so-called minority group are victimized by a person or group of men from within their group, they are often concerned about raising the issue for fear of fueling white culture's bigoted ideas of that minority group (for example, "Black men are so violent" or "What would you expect from a Mexican?"). If they are attacked by someone of the dominant group, they are legitimately concerned that acknowledging the attack will only bring recrimination against them in other ways. Furthermore, due to the racism of our culture, survivors of color are not likely to receive an appropriate and supportive response by the legal system, and often are held to higher standards in order to prove that what they experienced was victimization.

## SOCIETAL TRAUMA

Rape is also profoundly traumatic on a societal level. The "social trauma" is much less measurable, but is no less real. Women are not as free as men: Many women report adjusting their lives in dramatic ways as a result of the threat, and the reality, of rape. Women report being afraid whenever they go out at night, to the point that many women simply don't go out at night at all. In *The Female Fear*, Margaret Gordon and Stephanie Riger looked at the ways that women adjust their lives as a direct result of the fear of violence. What they found is very telling, and is something that those of us who are men need to pay special attention to. Some of what they found:

- 25 percent of women report that they do not walk in *their own neighborhood* after dark, as compared with 3 percent of men.

- 68 percent of women don't go to bars/clubs after dark, and three out of four women don't go to the movies—compared with 5 percent and one out of three men respectively.

- Almost one of two women don't use public transit after dark—as compared with one in four men.

- Over half of women won't go to parks alone after dark, while one in ten men won't.

- Finally, almost half of the women surveyed said they didn't go downtown after dark, compared with 7 percent of the men (p.15).

These statistics represent a world in which many of us, women *and* men, limit our activities because we don't feel safe. However, it also represents a world in which women feel more threatened, and are in greater danger than men—and a world in which women go to greater extremes and limit their lives in more severe ways than do men.

Imagine living a world in which you aren't safe anywhere, a world in which it isn't safe to walk to your neighborhood store at night for a gallon of milk. Then imagine not having a choice. Imagine being poor or barely surviving financially and even though you live in an "unsafe" neighborhood and even though it is 11:00 P.M., and even though there have been five reported rapes in your neighborhood over the past month—you still have to go to work because if you don't go to work you don't get paid and you have to use the bus because a taxi is outrageously expensive (even if you can get them to come into your neighborhood), and besides, that ten dollars represents tomorrow's dinner. Imagine feeling this level of terror every time you walk out your door, and having to swallow that fear. And now imagine living in a place where even though all those horrible conditions are true, out in the street, and you do feel entirely unsafe whenever you leave your home, it's still safer than being in your own home—and the men on the street that you fear are much safer than the men in your life. Most rapes are committed by the men who are in women's lives and homes—*not* on the streets by strangers. *This* is the political-societal context in which women live their lives.

What these numbers also mean is that the women *in our lives* are living their lives under certain restrictions that men don't have because they, as women, are afraid, and because we are men and have male privilege. The pervasiveness of the fear of men's violence means that the women with whom we live, study, work, and play—the women we care about and the women we share our lives with—all have to take extraordinary means in order to feel safe (if "ordinary" is taken to mean men's behaviors)—and they still don't. These numbers mean that women are thinking about this fear when they schedule classes, go to job interviews, look for places to live, and consider meeting us, their friends, at the movies or for dinner.

Tragically, what we know to be true about rape is that, despite these extreme lengths, women still *are not safe*. Women are still sexually victimized, and are still afraid. Think about it—*feel* about it. Women, as a class, in order to feel safe, have to adjust their lives thousands of ways every day in order to be safe, and they still aren't. The only way for women to be truly free from the threat of men's violence is to stay away from men. Many women don't have the luxury of taking into consideration how safe they may or may not be when looking for work. Additionally, as I've already discussed, women of color, children and adolescent women, and lesbian and bisexual women are at greater risk for being victimized than are women of privilege. They are also less likely to be believed and supported by the overwhelmingly white, heterosexual, and male "authorities" than are women of privilege. (This isn't to suggest that the "authorities" are necessarily appropriate or supportive of women of privilege when they are victimized).

### Rape as a Hate Crime

Sexual assault is a hate crime. It is used by a class of people (men) to maintain a position of domination over another class of people (women). The impact of sexual assault on individual women and men, as well as on women as a class, is similar to the impact on survivors of other kinds of hate violence. Further, the underlying attitudes that hold women as a class in less esteem than men as a class are parallel to the underlying attitudes of racism, heterosexism, and anti-Semitism that support racist attacks, homophobic violence, and religion-based viciousness.

Women are attacked precisely because they are women. The impact of sexual violence and the constant threat thereof is to keep women as a class "in their place." It is not coincidental that women are sexually victimized and are less likely to receive an adequate salary; that men rape and that men hold 90 percent of the seats of power in Congress and the White House; that women are afraid to go out at night and don't sit in the boardrooms of our nation's businesses. Sexual assault is acting out women-hate the same way that racist violence is acting out race-hate. In both cases the underlying hatred, which undergirds and justifies the violence, is endemic in our culture. The frequency of men's violence means that individual men don't necessarily have to use or threaten to use actual violence in order to control and dominate women.

## Men Are Raped Also

Men are sexually assaulted as well—almost always by other men and usually by heterosexual men. The personal trauma that men experience is still personal trauma. It affects them, like women, to the very core of who they are. Healing from being sexually victimized is still a life-long process. But on the societal level, the sexual assault of men has less to do with them as "men" and more to do with punishing them because they are or are perceived to be "deviant" from the image that our culture thinks of as a "man." Men who are raped describe feeling "emasculated" (i.e., made into a woman). Sexual assault of men is an attempt to feminize them (note the inherent misogyny of this statement—that being "feminized" is inherently a put-down for men)—and this continues to reinforce the inherent notion of women as being less than men—less valuable, less important, and less harmed by rape than are men. As has been stated in situations too numerous to count, "men aren't supposed to be raped." So, who is "supposed to be" raped? The statistics answer that question.

Statistically, men of color and gay or bisexual men are disproportionately sexually victimized. Men of color and queer men are traditionally and systematically emasculated by the racist and heterosexist notions of what "being a man" means. Look to our models: John Wayne, Rambo, Jean Claude Van Damme. All three are big, tough, isolated men. But all three are also white and blatantly heterosexual. This is the image of "being a man" in our culture. By definition, men of color and queer men cannot live up to that image.

The most frequent places where men are sexually assaulted are in prison, in the military, and in fraternities—all three of which were developed and are maintained to sustain a social structure of male supremacy. Rape occurring within these structures is only one example of the weapons they use to continue male supremacy. Men in prison who are set up as the target for systematic rape are frequently labeled as the "bitch" or the "woman" and kept subordinate in the hierarchy of prison life.

Fraternities are also notorious. At one fraternity at a large midwestern university, for example, the rush participants were sexually assaulted in a number of ways by gangs of their soon-to-be upper-class "brothers."* The attacks included verbal abuse of the victims referring to them as "little women," "girls," and "wusses," and occurred frequently over a period of a week or so. During this time, they were expected to act out their subordinate position as the "women" of the frat by acting out in exaggerated female stereotypes. After the series of attacks, they were told to go "do to women what we did to you to get your manhood back." As if that weren't bad enough, the fraternity would often then set women up during the rush party to be gang raped by the new members.

It is not my intention to bash fraternities. And I must acknowledge that this is an extreme case. But extreme cases expose the underlying prevalence of an attitude. In countless ways these same attitudes are expressed by men in whatever way we may gather together. Men in fraternities, men in dorms, men in business, men in the military—all express the same kinds of hatred towards women and disgust at any effeminate characteristics in men.

Rape is something that women are forced to think about, feel about, deal with, shape their lives around, and develop their consciousness about in ways that men simply do not, and probably cannot understand. It is difficult for men to comprehend, but something that we can begin to grasp—if we listen to the words of women.

Perhaps more eloquently than any other, Ntozake Shange has described the threatening reality of rape for women. This excerpt from the poem *with no immediate cause*, can be found in her book *Nappy Edges*:

> every 3 minutes a woman is beaten
> every five minutes a
> woman is raped/every ten minutes
> a little girl is molested
> yet I rode the subway today
> I sat next to an old man who

---

*This case was brought to my attention while on tour in 1990. For a number of reasons, I am forced to maintain the anonymity of the fraternity and the university.

may have beaten his old wife
3 minutes ago or 3 days/30 years ago
he might have sodomized his
daughter but I sat there

...

before I ride the subway/buy a paper or drink
coffee from your hands I must know
have you hurt a woman today
did you beat a woman today
throw a child cross a room are they
little girls pants in your pocket
did you hurt a woman today
I have to ask these obscene questions
I must know you see
the authorities require us to
establish

immediate cause
every three minutes
every five minutes
every ten minutes
every day.

## EFFECTS ON MEN

I know that is a very difficult and painful poem to read. It hurts. The
depth of Shange's feelings and her rage; the intensity with which she
describes these feelings; as well as the depth of our own feelings, which
are touched by this poem, mean it's probably very hard for you to sit still
right now. If you are like most men, you are probably feeling a great deal:
a mix of anger, frustration, hurt, despair, sadness, some shame and guilt,
maybe some hate. I know I am. You are also likely feeling some level(s) of
defensiveness. It's really difficult to read what Ntozake Shange wrote.
Those words are painful—and the reality they represent is horrific. It's
important for us, as men, to recognize and acknowledge the feelings that
come from a deep and honest discussion about sexual violence.

Unfortunately, for the most part, male training has kept us from
learning the skills of identifying, labeling, and expressing our feelings. This
is a great opportunity to learn some of those skills. I'd like to suggest that
you try an exercise. Take a break from reading this book, grab a pad of
paper and a pen, and begin writing. Don't think about what you're writing,
just write. Write about what is happening in your body: in the pit of your

stomach, in your neck, around your heart, in your groin area, in your throat; describe the feelings you have—even if you don't have the language to label what is happening, write. Try writing with your non-dominant hand (i.e., if you're right-handed, write with your left hand, and vice versa). This technique can help you break through the pattern of thinking about what you're writing.

If you can, identify any guilt and shame that you may be feeling and tease those feelings out. They don't help, and do nothing to stop rape. To borrow from Robin Morgan (talking about blame), "in addition to being counterproductive and boring, it isn't the point"—and, I would add, is a waste of time and energy. Guilt and shame only work to keep your attention on yourself, keep you powerless, keep you from looking towards effective solutions, and destroy your self-image.

It's important to critically examine ourselves and what we base our self-image on, but tearing ourselves down is useless! I'm not saying this self-examination is easy—but it is necessary. It is essential to have and create space for your feelings and to share the feelings you're experiencing. But you also have the ability to choose which feelings you focus on, and how to express your feelings. You may, for example, be feeling sad and powerless—but it's easier to express guilt and so that's what you present—that's how you respond to these words. Regardless of where it comes from, you *do* have the ability to identify the guilt feelings and separate those from the others. Then, focus on those others using them as motivation and energy to change. If you're angry at the idea that women perceive you as a threat, try to direct that anger at the pervasiveness of men's violence that drives those perceptions. Use your anger as fuel for change.

If you don't feel blamed, guilty, or ashamed, you will have little reason to feel defensive. Men, collectively, haven't responded to rape. There have always been individual men (painfully few, but we must acknowledge that they do exist) who have acted in support of feminists and have refused to keep silent. I'm not attacking men—and neither, I believe, is Ntozake Shange. Rather, we are trying to paint an honest and poignant picture of reality—in a way that you can see. This reality is ugly; it's painful and it's hard to look at. The reality is that men are violent against women. Any man can, and many men do, choose to be violent with near impunity. For most men, violence and sex has become intertwined. And almost all of us who choose not to be violent are conspiratorially silent about the violence that our brothers are perpetrating. If you feel guilty about that, then read on, and learn to do something to "break the silence and end men's violence."

Now, if you will, put any defensiveness that may be coming to the surface for you on hold. I'm not saying to deny that it is there. Rather, recognize it, and put it up on a shelf for a moment. As you read on, you very well may find that there isn't any reason for it. Look at where Shange's anger is coming from. If you can, try to connect with her anger and her rage. A part of defensiveness comes from feeling like we're supposed to "make it all better" but not having the slightest clue how to begin or what to do. The most important thing you can "do" right now is to acknowledge the truth, and listen to women's experience.

One of the greatest assets of anger is when we use it as an ally and a friend, and direct that incredibly powerful emotion towards change. A great deal of my energy comes from anger. I'm angry at the way the world is, the way that women and children are treated, the way that I'm told to "be a man" and the lack of validity when I cannot or choose not to live up to those standards. I can either choose to direct that anger at feminists for their "man-hating" (sic), or focus this anger productively to create a world where there isn't any woman-hating and therefore I won't be perceived as a threat. We can choose to use our anger as the motivating energy to create a world where women and men can truly, finally, be allies and partners, as we were meant to be.

Expressing how we feel is a beginning towards interrupting the male patterns that support rape, and thus, a way to begin stopping rape. Even beyond empathizing with women, children, and rape survivors, men need to articulate the ways rape impacts on us. I'm in no way suggesting that the pain we feel compares in any way to the pain and oppression that women experience. But each and every one of us is deeply, profoundly, and personally affected by rape. Beyond having women and men in our lives who have been victimized, even beyond being aware that most (if not all) of us have perpetrated sexist and abusive behaviors, all of us are looked at by women who are questioning, "Have you hurt a woman today?" Each and every one of us has been and is being seen and responded to as a threat—a potential rapist. How are women to know the difference? Seeing you ride on the subway to work reading this book, how is the woman sitting across from you supposed to know that you are a "safe" man and not someone who is likely to follow her and attack her?

Every three minutes a woman is battered, and how are the women sitting next to you on the subway, working in the cubicle next to you, or with whom you are flirting at the bar, supposed to know that you aren't one of "those" men? No telltale signs differentiate men who rape, batter, or molest children from the rest of us. No way exists to tell the difference between "those" men who rape, and "us" men who wouldn't or "don't."

That dichotomy itself is a falsehood, and is not helpful to working to stop rape. There are no "good" men and no "bad" men. There are only men—and all of us do some good things, and some not-so-good things. The men that women fear are us. It is me as I sit in my living room writing this book, it is me on my way to Howard University to offer a presentation, it is me sitting on the train going to Boston. It is you sitting on the bus reading this book on your way to work, it is you making your way to class or the library. The men that are most dangerous to women are us, and the men women fear are us. That's one of the crucial concepts that we need to begin working on this issue. Men, rape affects *us* too!

Beyond the men who survive rape, and those who are involved in relationships of one kind or another with someone who has survived, rape impacts all men. Because some men use their penises as a weapon, and because there is no way to distinguish these men from other men, all men are suspect. Even if we are unaware, in a cognitive way, of being seen constantly by women and most children as a threat, it seems clear that we are aware on some level. This awareness has an impact on our self-esteem. It is difficult to feel good about ourselves as human beings when well over half the human race is frightened of us—with good reason.

What this dynamic exposes is the extreme extent to which men are separated from the rest of humankind and the planet on which we live. We could not be this violent, or tolerate the extent of the violence, if we felt connected to women, children, each other, and the planet. We know this lack of connection comes in part from the militaristic mindset that permeates our culture. You must create and dehumanize an "enemy" before you are able to make war or tolerate the violence of war. In order to continue to turn a blind eye to rape, battery, incest, the pain, the oppression, and the violence, you must detach yourself from the humanity of the people being victimized. Disconnecting from our own feelings, other people, and the planet is the first step in teaching men to be "men," *and* in teaching men to rape. That is an incredibly destructive pattern. Clearly it's destructive to other people and to our entire planet. But it is also destructive to ourselves. Dissociating in this way removes us from humanity. You can't feel good about yourself and be isolated. But in order to "be men" we're supposed to be "independent." The models that we have of "manly men" (John Wayne, Rambo, and Jean Claude Van Damme) are also men who are all but totally isolated.

Furthermore, men are taught that one of our primary roles is to protect "our" women and children. Too often, the fear that many men have of other men attacking the women we love is expressed in jealous, possessive, and controlling behaviors toward the women we love—in the name of "keeping them safe." The men who we are protecting "our" women from are our brothers, our friends, and our neighbors. Ironically, we are "protecting" women and children from the very men that we should be becoming closest with. By definition, this creates a situation where we must maintain some distance between ourselves and other men. After all, he just might be one of "those" men. But this situation also reinforces the distance between men and the women in our lives. How close can we get to somebody if we are supposed to be always "looking out for their best interests" and being aware of any threat? We live in a time when men are reporting feeling very isolated and lonely. We can't reconnect with ourselves or with others as long as rape continues to be a threat that we are not responding to directly and effectively.

If as many women are being victimized as I've just reported (and this is a gross *under*estimation of the total amount of victimization), then how many men are doing the victimizing? The truth of the matter is that we simply don't know! We *do* know that most men convicted of sexual assaults have committed a number of sexual attacks. But given how common it is for women and men to be sexually victimized—from sexual and gender harassment up to and including gang rape and femicide (the killing of women because they are women), it seems that large numbers of us are sexually victimizing. Even if we don't directly victimize women or other men, we likely know men who have, and who do.

We get a further suggestion of the number of men who sexually assault by examining the research that asks exactly that question. When men on college campuses all over this country are asked if they would rape if they could get away with it, anywhere from 15 to 27 percent say they would. When the phrasing of the question is changed from "rape" to "force a woman to have sex against her will" (which is still rape), the number of men who say they would ("if they knew they would get away with it") jumps to as high as *60 percent*. This research has been duplicated numerous times. In *I Never Called It Rape*, Robin Warshaw found that:

- 91.3 percent of men said they "enjoyed dominating women."

- 63.5 percent said they "get excited when a woman struggles over sex."

- 61.7 percent said they thought it "would be exciting to use force to subdue a woman" (p.93).

(I was unable to find any information anywhere that looked at men's attitudes towards forcing men to have sex, or towards the issue of male rape in any form).

Given the ubiquity of these attitudes, it quickly becomes obvious that there are men in our lives who are victimizing. As I stated earlier, the men who are raping the women in our lives are the men in our lives. We need to stop looking at "those" men, "those sickos," "those wierdos" as the rapists and to take full responsibility for rape. We need to begin looking at our own selves—for it *is* us. Acknowledging that it is our friends and maybe ourselves who sexually victimize women can be more scary and painful than acknowledging the incidence of rape for women and men.

It's a necessary step to see just how common rape is, to identify and expose the "subtle" expressions of the attitudes that encourage sexual assault, and to acknowledge what we know about supporting rape attitudes. Regardless of how many men actually do rape, the idea that a man can get off on sexual coercion/force/violence comes from somewhere. Somehow, some (some, many, most, all, one) men get the idea that sexual victimization (sexual assault, rape, harassment) is acceptable. Stopping rape requires that men find out and expose the ways that men get these ideas from our culture.

We all come from a similar male culture. Regardless of our ethnic background, we, as men, grow up in this culture learning many of the same basic messages about being men. While some major differences exist between men of different cultures, of different ages, of different sexual orientations, and of different religions, masculinity still maintains some basic tenets. Men from every class, race, sexual orientation, religion, and culture rape. Rape comes from the culture of masculinity. The only way that we have a chance to stop rape is for each of us as men to deconstruct masculinity from within our own culture and identify, expose, and eliminate those tenets of masculinity that support rape. At the same time, we have to work to redefine masculinity in a way that is about liberation, freedom, and nonviolence.

By getting together as men, man to man, and discussing these issues, we can begin uncovering what we do know and exposing these connections. In fact, that is the only way. We won't uncover these issues and recognize these truths in isolation. We have to come together and work together in order to develop our understanding and identify effective ways to tell these truths. We all have ideas about the connections between "being a man" and sexual violence: the ways that "being a man"—taking control, taking charge, deciding what we want and going for it at all costs, being noncommunicative, and keeping a score—set us up for sexually abusing behaviors. As we get better about talking about these issues and the ways they affect our lives, we will also become better able to expose these connections and begin undermining the culture of rape.

There is a difference between a person and his behavior. The men who rape, harass, or act in sexist ways are not bad or wrong or evil. Their *behavior* is. The men themselves very well may be decent guys. They may also be scums of the earth. For example, to be honest, I need to acknowledge that many of my early sexual experiences were full of abusive, manipulative, and controlling dynamics. Looking back from where I sit now, I would have to identify some of my early sexual experiences as rape. I know that throughout high school and into college, I participated in a lot of harassing behaviors against women—it was one of the main ways that I bonded with my male friends. None of those behaviors make me an evil person. Saying that in no way lets me off the hook for the people that I hurt. But it doesn't mean I'm a "bad" person. Similarly, writing this book and doing anti-rape work does not make me a "good" person. Writing this book, which is a good thing, is a behavior; it is not me. Harassing or abusing women was a behavior—a behavior that I am completely and solely responsible for, but a behavior that is distinct from my innate humanity.

Furthermore, by painting "those" men as "evil" men, we effectively let them off the hook. They don't have to take responsibility for hurting somebody if they are "bad" people. If and when we acknowledge their full humanity, and recognize them as completely competent human beings, then they become completely responsible for the pain they have caused, and the abuse they have perpetrated. When I do something, intentionally or not, that is sexist or harassing, I and I alone am responsible for the pain or discomfort I caused. I am further responsible for working things out with the person I hurt. If I were just a "bad" person, I wouldn't necessarily have that responsibility because "I'm a bad person—what else do you expect?" That argument, in fact, was a part of the defense of Mike Tyson during his rape trial in early 1992. As a boxer and a man with a reputation for treating women badly, it was argued, any woman should have expected to be pressured for sex. That effectively lets him off the hook.

Additionally, by keeping men from taking full responsibility for *all* of our behavior, we are effectively portraying men as powerless to change. I refuse to allow men to be disempowered in this way. Being a liberated person, a fully empowered person, a completely competent human being, *requires* that we take full responsibility for our behaviors—the good, the neutral, and the inexcusable. When we do something hurtful or abusive, our friends have the obligation to confront us on our hurtful and abusive behaviors and we have an obligation to respond.

Along with the responsibility we have to our sisters—our mothers, sisters, friends, partners, and the women on the street—we have the responsibility to ourselves and to other men for creating a world in which not every man is seen as a threat, a potential rapist, and as violence and oppression personified.

TWO

# THE CULTURE
# OF RAPE

AS PERSONALLY TRAUMATIC as it is, rape is also a political crime
that occurs in a socio-cultural context. As I showed in the previous
chapter, rape is a hate crime. Rape is used as a weapon to maintain men's
position of dominance over women. Regardless of the intent of individual
men who rape, as a result all women have fewer opportunities. Men use
the fear, the threat, and the silence surrounding rape to keep ourselves in
a dominant position over women. We use the men who rape to paint
ourselves as "good" men who wouldn't rape and then argue that we
deserve the praise and support of women—basically because we don't do
something horrible to them. Whether or not all men rape, all men use rape
to stay "up" over women.

Our very culture supports and encourages rape. Feminists have for a
number of years categorized our culture as a "rape culture." What they
mean is that our culture supports and activey encourages men to rape
women, people of color, children, and gay men and lesbians. Our culture
creates an environment in which rape is not only normative, rape is
necessary.

The original rape laws in this country, some of which weren't changed
until the 1970s, defined the crime of rape and its penalties in terms of the
"crime" against the husband or father of the victim/survivor. His
"property" had been damaged. In fact, in most jurisdictions, the "rape"
laws were defined similarly to cattle theft. The legal system did not
conceive of it as a crime against the woman herself.

The history of the laws on wife-beating provide another paradigmatic
example of our rape culture. The original laws prohibiting wife beating in
this country were based on the English common law "rule of thumb,"

whereby a husband could beat his wife so long as the instrument he used was no bigger around than the width of his thumb. (Of course, she had no right to beat him.)

You may argue that we have come a long way from the society that these laws represent (thanks to the efforts and organizing of feminists). And it's true, we have come a long way—to some extent. But what does it mean when our entire legal system is based on these ideas? It may be fine-tuned and adjusted. But the mindset on which these laws were based continues, for example, in the contemporary "joke," "If you can't rape your wife, who can you rape?" It's the same mindset that asks, "Why did she agree to go out with him?" "Why does she stay?" "Why was she wearing *that*?" This mindset is still alive and active in our society. Further, this mindset is reinforced by our culture, for example, through endless media images that portray women as culpable in their victimizations.

Here's an example of how all men benefit from rape culture. Remembering the statistics on the ways that women adjust their lives as a result of the threat of rape how do women run for public office? You may say that these two ideas aren't related, but how are you supposed to run for office when it's unsafe to go out at night? We who claim that we are against rape use that false dichotomy (the "bad" men who rape and the "good" men who don't) to paint ourselves as the "allies" of women and continue to keep getting ourselves elected to office to maintain access to women's bodies, and to continue to receive women's praise. After all, "they need us."

Our culture begins with the assumption that "man" is the center of the universe. This is probably best described by looking at our use of language: "man"-kind, Congress-"men," God the "father," the use of the "generic" he, his, etc. "He" is the center, she is an afterthought. As an afterthought, what happens to her isn't quite as important. Any violence or oppression that happens to her is more easily justifiable. For example, try the following exercise. Try using the female pronouns as generic just for one day. Try talking about womankind, and firewomen, policewomen, Congresswomen, God the mother, and using the "generic" she and her. It won't be easy, but try. As you try, notice your own reactions as well as the responses of people around you. Listen to how people argue that you're making assumptions and "how do you know she's a she?" Notice what happens and the ways that you feel excluded. Notice the mind games you are forced to play in order to include yourself in the dialogue. Finally, remember that women have to do that *all the time*.

When you don't count enough to even be recognized in our daily conversations and interactions, how can you claim to count enough to be cared for when something bad is done to you? Women have been effectively written out of our consciousness. When they don't exist, or when they exist only as "other," it becomes possible to victimize them with relative impunity. We have come to conceptualize "them" (women, people of color, gays and bi's) as different, as "other." In that mindset, violation becomes par for the course.

It is important to define (and redefine) what "being a man" means—for it is more than simply having a penis, testosterone, or a Y chromosome. "Being a man" in our culture means not only being male but also being adult (but not "old"), white, heterosexual, and able-bodied. "Being a man" means living up to the John Wayne or Rambo image of, to quote bell hooks, "phallocentric masculinity"—the entire definition of who we are as human beings is based on the power and privilege we are granted because we have a penis. "Being a man" is based on having a penis, but gets immediately tangled up with sexist, racist, heterosexist, ageist, and able-ist notions such as being rational, clear thinking, and logical (which have developed into being emotionally detached, cold, and inflexible); being in control and making the decisions; and seeing what we want and "going for it" regardless of the potential costs. The move from this place is to raping is not far. Being "rational and logical" becomes "you agreed to go out with me and come over for a nightcap . . . logically you agreed to have sex with me." Being "in control" and making all the decisions becomes "I'll call you at seven, pick you up at eight-thirty, I'll drive, we'll go to the movies and to dinner, then we'll come back here and have sex . . . ." Seeing what we want and "going for it" becomes "I'm going to have her . . . ."

When taken out of the interpersonal realm and placed into a cultural context, these conceptions become the political, social, cultural and economic system of patriarchy. Patriarchy, as defined by feminists, is the process of using the system of male supremacy found in traditional families (i.e., the "father's house") as a paradigm for the world order. Patriarchy is a system in which men create the definitions of power, the ways to maintain power, and the avenues for obtaining power in all of its forms. For example, power has come to mean something that is external from us, that is in limited supply, and that is always conceived as a power "over" other people. The examples are endless: political, economic, militaristic, educational, religious or spiritual, industrial, scientific, etc. Men, traditionally and currently, hold the seats of "power" in all of these areas, through roles such as heads of state, high church authorities, corporate boardmembers, principles, college presidents, judges and police chiefs.

We have then created processes to make sure that we maintain ourselves in those "power over" positions. We may have offered people who have traditionally been disenfranchised equal opportunity to *apply* to those positions of power (which requires that they too adopt the same conceptualization of power), but we continue to block any attempts to equal opportunity to *get* those positions of power.*

Patriarchy takes the biological differences of male (having a penis) and female (having a vagina) and imposes social norms and mores onto those physiological forms creating "man" and "woman." According to this socially created reality, males and females are biologically, physiologically, and chemically different from one another. Culture then uses those differences as the basis for expected differences in social behavior. This notion, I believe, is damaging or harmful in its own right. This artificial distinction creates a world of misunderstanding and a chasm of differences that is difficult, if not impossible, to cross.

The physiological differences do exist. However, as Marilyn French noted in *Beyond Power*, "Sexual dimorphism—a difference in form and size between the two sexes—does not lead to the dominance or domination of the larger sex"(p.30). While gender differences may exist, male domination is created. Behavioral differences, most (if not all) of which are socially constructed, are exaggerated to the point of absurdity, creating a barrier that keeps all of us from our true and full humanity. All of us have been taught that women and men are "opposites" and that certain behaviors are "just male" and certain others are "just female." For example, childcare, housecleaning, and nursing are roles for women, while coaching, yardwork, and roles of violence are assigned to men. Little opportunity is left to share, to learn, and tointerrelate between these falsely created chasms.

Patriarchy then goes on to place these socially constructed and exaggerated differences into a hierarchy where those qualities associated with maleness are valued most. There is no evidence to support this hierarchy as "natural" or true because these differences are just that—differences. Difference does not inherently include a better or worse, just a distinction. However, most of us have internalized patriarchal thinking so completely that it is difficult to conceive of differences without putting them on a scale of better or worse. According to Nelle

---

*Thanks to Sandra Crewe for first articulating this understanding for me.

Morton in "Toward a Whole Theology"(unpublished), we perceive a world which is divided into "good/evil, redemption/guilt, authority/obedience, reward/punishment, power/powerlessness, haves/havenots, and master/slave." I would add to her list male/female, white/black, heterosexual/ homosexual, and normal/sick.

Within this hierarchy and these false dichotomies, the world gets divided between "mankind" (which also means people of European descent, heterosexuals, and adults), and un-mankind (women; people of color; lesbians, homosexuals and bisexuals; and children). As such, patriarchy maintains not only male supremacy but white supremacy as well. Helen Zia found, not coincidentally, that most white supremacist groups also espouse a hatred of feminism, the maintenance of traditional gender roles, and male domination. Patriarchy additionally supports and maintains adult, heterosexual, and other forms of supremacy, all based upon a hierarchy of difference in which differences are judged and exaggerated to justify mistreatment, abuse, and oppression.

In patriarchy each individual man, regardless of how opposed to patriarchy he may personally be, represents a system in which women and other "un-men" are exploited, oppressed, dominated, and even killed because they do not belong to the class of "man." According to patriarchy, only man has any value. Un-men have no value, and you can exploit what doesn't have any value. History gives us countless examples: Whites were legally allowed and encouraged to exploit Blacks because Blacks were perceived as only three-fifths human in the original U.S. Constitution. Identified as "savages" and thus perceived of as less than fully human, Native Americans were slaughtered for the first several centuries after Columbus landed on these shores. Children have never been seen as fully human; they have no voice in government, and a child is defined as the property of her or his parents according to the law. Yet ten children die every day in this country at the hands of their parents. Gay men, lesbians, and bisexuals are seen as "not normal," in other words, not heterosexual, and thus are not seen as being worthy of the same rights as heterosexuals. So gay-bashing and even murder is justified, minimized, or ignored. And women are seen as "less than" men and so the fact that they are raped, assaulted, harassed, and killed is not taken seriously.

In *Our Blood*, Andrea Dworkin first identified and articulated the difference between truth and reality.* The reality is the socially

---

*I cannot adequately express my debt and gratitude to the tireless work of Andrea Dworkin. Her writing, organizing, and efforts on behalf of women have been an ongoing inspiration

constructed misinformation identified above. The truth is that males and
females, on the physiological and biochemical level, actually exist on a
continuum. On one extreme is male and on the other is female. Most of
us fall somewhere in middle, merging the two. For example, the penis is
structurally little more than an extended clitoris, testicles little different
than vaginal walls. Additionally, we all have extremely variant levels of
estrogen and testosterone—the chemicals thought to be responsible for
some of the differences between being female and being male. John
Stoltenberg writes,

> Sexuality does not *have* a gender, it *creates* a gender. It creates for those
> who adapt to it in narrow and specified ways the confirmation for the
> individual of belonging to the idea of one sex or the other. To achieve
> male sexual identity requires that an individual *identify with* the class of
> males (p.33).

Male identity "also requires *nonidentification with* that which is
perceived to be non-male, or female. His identity 'as a man' absolutely
depends on the extent to which he repudiates the values and interests of
womankind" (p. 34).

## MALE PRIVILEGE

Even though many men do not rape (I'm referring specifically to the
legal definition here, and base this statement on the assumption that the
available statistics are correct even though most men have probably forced
sex), and many are probably opposed to rape, all men benefit from rape
and the constant threat of rape. If we benefit in no other way, we at least
don't live with the constant threat of rape. Rape affects *every* woman's life.
Not only are 42 percent of women directly victimized (Russell 1984,
p.35), but all women are threatened, controlled, and victimized by the
reality of rape and the constant threat that exists—represented by every
man.

Furthermore, most if not all women are victimized by harassment and
other forms of sexist acts. In order to minimize the amount of
victimization, women must learn to look at all men with suspicion. There
is always the question of whether "this man" may be one of "those men."
Even if the man doesn't overtly threaten her, the fact is that some men do,

---

and source of immense awe for me. I wouldn't have come to most of what I understand to
be true if it weren't for the work of Andrea Dworkin.

and she doesn't know whether this particular man is one of the men who may.

Most women are raped by men they know and trust. There is no way to determine which man may be a rapist or which man is not. As such, men are able to benefit from a system that keeps women in a position of relative defensiveness and fear. Men can walk with much more freedom and independence than can women, and that we can is a direct result of rape as a threat, and a reality. Because of this, rape becomes a weapon of male supremacy which simultaneously maintains male supremacy.

Men benefit from patriarchy, and from the political crime and personal trauma of rape, regardless of how actively we participate in that system or how supportive we may be of patriarchy. We benefit in countless ways, many of which we aren't even aware of as benefits. For example, men are free(er) to walk down any streets we choose and not fear the threat of men's violence. This isn't entirely true, as men also are victimized by male violence. Additionally, men of color, gay and bi men, and male children do have streets that are off-limits to them. Overwhelmingly, this violence too is perpetrated by men, and the fear that springs from the threat of this violence is fear of men. Furthermore, men of whatever social group are less vulnerable and less fearful than are women of the same group.

But there are other benefits to patriarchy as well. Men have the choice of taking off our shirts when we are hot. Men are able to look to positions of patriarchially defined "power" and see our own images mirrored back (mostly true for white men, but always more true for the men of any social group than for the women of the same group). We can work without the fear of losing our jobs for refusing the advances of our boss. We can trust that we will be able to make a decent living with whatever jobs we have.

Perhaps the most basic benefit men receive as a result of rape and rape culture is that we are guaranteed a position or a role to play. Traditional masculinity has defined men's role as that of protector of "his" women and "his" family. As societies have developed, the clear threats to "our" women and family are less identifiable. Yet our culture still maintains and reinforces those old worn-out images and definitions of masculinity (the latest incarnation being the "mytho-poetic" or "male fundamentalist" movement).* As such, men need to have some threat to "our" women in order to justify our existence. Rape acts as that threat. Those of us who

---

*Thanks to Martin DeFresne who first came up with this very apt description of the mytho-poetic movement.

allegedly wouldn't rape, who are supposedly opposed to rape, benefit because we are then defined as the "good" men.

All men benefit because, as long as women are kept in a subordinate position, men keep our position of dominance—whether or not we personally choose to support the system, or if we want to stay in that position. Rape is one of the weapons used to keep women subordinate. For example, I've had the opportunity to speak all over the U.S., in Canada, and several other countries. This is a prime example of male privilege, for I am approached not just because what I have to say is so important, but also because I am a *man* saying these things. Countless women say the same things and aren't invited to speak. This is an example of, among other dynamics, male privilege—of me, a man, using the benefits that I am offered because I happen to have been born with a penis. This isn't to necessarily say that our contributions as men are any less valuable. But it adds a level of complexity and honesty to the discussion. There are lots of contradictions and paradoxes to men doing anti-rape work.

When we express the benefits we receive due to living in a culture that values those with penises more than those without, we remind women of the "power" that we have access to: the power and threat to commit rape. It is just this kind of power differential that, taken to its not-so-extreme, becomes rape and other forms of men's violence. Rape is an expression of male privilege as well as an expression of violence, hatred, domination, and a host of other things. But as an expression of male privilege, rape reinforces our system of male supremacy and domination over women. In order to eliminate rape, we must confront this power differential.

In summary, several aspects are key in the maintenance of male supremacy. One element is to define women as fitting only very specific and limited roles. Another is to use sexist language that excludes women and creates an image for the audience which is limited to only men. Pornography defines women as an object of sex, and as deserving whatever she gets. Rape limits the lives of women in ways too countless to name. Regardless of the specific form of male privilege that men express, it reminds women of the connection to the other expressions that men could choose (all violence is a choice, and living an anti-sexist lifestyle is a choice) to express—and some of those expressions are deadly for women. We are in complete control of how we choose to express our connection to male power, male privilege.

### Supporting Rape Culture

As men, we all support rape culture. The most blatant examples include denying women's definition of rape or minimizing the impact that rape has on the lives of women and men who have survived. More subtle examples include not responding to the issues of rape in general, or maintaining a safe and convenient silence around the subject. Other behaviors, which many men feel are much more subtle, are used on a frequent basis. These behaviors, expressed by attitude or by language usage, support rape in that they support a system which denigrates and limits women. Further, these subtler behaviors support a system in which men are dominant, and women are submissive. It is just such a system (individual, interpersonal, small-group, or societal) in which rape occurs. It is the same attitudes and beliefs that support a larger system of male control and domination that also support rape.

Examining some of men's terms for issues surrounding sex and sexuality can give us a glimpse of these kinds of attitudes:

⁰ the ways men refer to sex:
  "scoring"
  "banging"
  "fucking"

⁰ the ways men refer to women with whom they have sex:
  "whore"
  "cunt"
  "piece"

⁰ the ways men refer to female genitalia:
  "hole"
  "pussy"
  "cunt"

⁰ the ways men refer to male genitalia:
  "dick"
  "cock"
  "love stick"
  "sword"

Consider the violent and predator/prey symbolism of this kind of language. This language and mentality circulate within the context of a culture in which almost nine out of ten women are sexually victimized in their lifetime. Not only that, this is a language and mentality that all of us as men have been raised to understand and use.

## The Legal System

The legal system is the basis for most of our interactions in U.S. culture. We base many of our interactions on some level of understanding and internalizing of the legal system. In relation to rape, for example, the law draws a line between what is rape and what isn't. Most men want to know precisely where that line is drawn. Many are not aware that many more abusive and hurtful behaviors don't cross the legal line, but are still abusive.

Additionally, the legal system in the U.S. was created by men to protect and maintain abuse and domination. It was not created to protect or encourage civil rights (if it were, we wouldn't have such an incredible struggle to expand, strengthen, and enforce those rights); it was created and continues in order to protect male (and white, heterosexual, and adult) superiority.

Those in power in the legal system see issues concerned with the "other" as unimportant. Women are seen as "other" and rape is seen as a "women's issue." Therefore, the men in power don't address rape appropriately. Currently, men write the rape laws (the vast majority of state legislators and Congress is male), enforce the rape laws (most police officers are male), interpret the rape laws (most lawyers are male), judge the accused and the victim-survivors (most judges are male), and rape (as has been discussed, the vast majority of rapists are male). I don't want to fuel conspiracy theories about rape, but this framework looks more than a little disconcerting. It mirrors the reality of other dispossessed populations: people of color, gays and lesbians, the poor. Additionally, because men are in these positions, and all men grow up in the dominant culture that prepares males to "be men," all men in these positions of power know only too well and only too internally these rape attitudes.*

It is not an accident, nor is it coincidental, that women are raped and women make up six of a hundred senators; forty-eight of the 436 members of the House of Representatives; one of nine Supreme Court Justices; and we've never had a woman as a major candidate for president. And rape has never been an election issue. It is not a coincidence that women are sexually harassed in the workplace and the classroom and still are making sixty-nine cents for every dollar a man makes. Furthermore, when these realities are then put into the racist and heterosexist political context within which we all live, the double and triple jeopardy for women of color and lesbian and bisexual women becomes even clearer.

---

*For a more complete discussion of this issue, see *Pornography and Civil Rights: A New Day for Women's Equality* (1988) by Andrea Dworkin and Catherine MacKinnon.

*Defining Patriarchy*

Patriarchy is a terrible, violent, vile system that destroys huge pieces of all of us—our individual humanness and humanness in general. Patriarchy creates men who choose to act oppressively and violently, who create huge systems of destruction and manage to find ways to "turn a profit" in the process, men who are distant and unfeeling, and men who aren't able to identify their feelings, much less express them. Patriarchy creates men who use and abuse alcohol and other drugs to excess, men who don't understand how to be with a child, men who hate their bodies and themselves.

Patriarchy likewise creates women who work at not making decisions, women who place others before themselves, women who are victimized countless times. Patriarchy creates women who are afraid to communicate honestly, and who don't know how to "be" unless it is "doing something." Patriarchy is a terrible and destructive system that hurts us all and from which none of us emerges unscathed.

However, there is a difference between hurt and oppression. Men and women, adults and children are all hurt, continuously, by patriarchy. This system reduces all of us to little more than a measure of how "effective" or "successful" we are or are not in playing out the societal rules of "being a man" or "being a woman." As a result, all of us lose major pieces of our full humanity: our total intelligence, our complete sensitivity, our unlimited creativity, our full beauty. In trying to live up to the definitions, we limit ourselves to the possibilities. All of us are hurt.

Women, on the other hand, are also oppressed by the system of male supremacy and by men. Women are living in a system in which they continue to make sixty-nine cents for every dollar a man makes; in which less than ten cents is spent on the health needs of women for every dollar that is spent for the health needs of men; in which more emphasis is put on stopping the drug trade than on identifying and responding to women's pain and victimization. Individual men are making these decisions. Furthermore, women are sexually harassed, raped, beaten, attacked, and killed by individual men, in a culture in which women-hate is a prominent value.

Patriarchy is a death system. It is a system based on destruction, violence, and degradation. Any such system is doomed to destroy itself. And in the meantime, it kills all of those who participate in such a system. For survival's sake, all of us need to work to end this deathly system. We have seen any number of revolutions occur, any number of social change movements come and go. Unfortunately, almost without exception, these revolutions have worked to revolutionize the symptom, without taking on the true root of oppression. Stopping rape—and in the process confronting patriarchy—is truly the form of radical social change that can result in the kinds of dramatic world alteration that many of us are looking for. When we succeed in stopping rape, we will have succeeded in altering our society in such a way as to make all other forms and examples of oppression obsolete. For those of us for whom social change is a force in our lives, for those of you who consider yourselves peace-niks, those of you who work for peace and social justice, it is imperative that we take on the responsibility of working to destroy patriarchy and to stop rape.

## ON BEING A "WOMAN": FEMININITY AND VULNERABILITY

Part of the theory of patriarchy is that women are the "weaker sex" (we've all heard this one). This view of women creates a perception of women being unable to care adequately for themselves and therefore "needing a man." Included in that stereotype is the assumption that men are the stronger gender and are able and willing to "protect" and "care for" women. This reinforces the power imbalance between women and men and maintains men in a "power over" position. Further, the assumption of women as weaker and therefore needing to be protected (from what?) casts women as less capable than men, and therefore more vulnerable. Tragically, this view of women as less capable tends to be internalized by women, which only magnifies their vulnerability. It is only a short step between being less capable and being less fully human. And, as I've already discussed, when one is less than human, exploitation can occur with relative impunity. In other words, it is the very position of "power over" and this view of women as needing to be protected and as less than fully human that—when coupled with the eroticization of power and control and taken to its logical conclusion—becomes rape.

Patriarchy goes on to define women as care-givers. According to patriarchy, women are supposed to take care of everybody—the husband or boyfriend, the children, the sick cat, the house, and the next-door neighbor before meeting their own needs. The pattern of putting their own needs last places women into a position of potential vulnerability, for it puts women into a position of waiting for others, particularly "her man," to act before she responds.* She is supposed to meet his needs, which

---

*By definition, this excludes women in same-sex relationships. According to the definitions promulgated by male supremacy, lesbians and bisexual women are even more invisible than

means that she must wait for him to define his needs before she can meet them. Inherent in this role is the expectation that she be passive, and this passivity puts women into the difficult position of not having the experience or training to assertively work to meet their own needs. Women are then in a position of hesitancy—not acting in a proactive or assertive manner. Additionally, when a dangerous situation arises, women then sometimes act out this training and react passively. She is, after all, supposed to "lie there and take it" and besides, "whatever happens is her fault anyway."

Women are also taught that "meeting his needs" includes meeting his sexual needs. The culture sees it as a woman's responsibility to meet the sexual needs of "her man." Consider the number of contraceptive devices that are invented for women as opposed to those invented for men (despite or because of the fact that most researchers are men), or the assumption that "she will be ready if I just . . . ." Together, these two expectations place women into a position of vulnerability, for men are supposed to push for sex, and women are supposed to ultimately "give in."

The difficulty lies in deciding where the line gets drawn, and who draws the line between "normal" sexual involvement and acquaintance rape, in which he "pushes too far?" For example, in 1992 the Pennsylvania Supreme Court voted that "no is not enough." In this decision, the court found that, even though the woman said no repeatedly, and left the room immediately after the attack, crying, she had not said no in a forceful enough manner. Thus, they threw out the rape charges. Who draws the line? Clearly she had drawn the line at one level of behavior, he drew a different line somewhere else, and the court supported his interpretation of where the line between rape and "normal" sexual involvement lies. So who do we believe when rape allegations are made? In my view, we should trust the person describing victimization and trauma before anyone else.

Furthermore, our society teaches women that they are "nothing without a man." Not that women are bad or wrong in some way, but that they "do not exist" without being attached to a man. (Anne Wilson Schaef discusses these issues more fully in her 1981 book, *Women's Reality*.) This lie clearly is played out in any number of ways. For example, in traditional U.S. naming practices, a woman goes from being "daddy's little girl" to her "husband's wife" without the opportunity to develop her own sense of self

---

heterosexual women, and don't even live up the identity of "woman." As such, their vulnerability is increased.

(or last name). Women are escorted down the aisle by their father to be "given to" their husband. Not only does this reinforce the notion that women are the chattel of men, but it also puts a woman at risk, for without an identity in her own right, what human rights does she have?

## ON BECOMING "MEN": PRO-RAPE TRAINING

In patriarchy, particularly as interpreted by American society, "man" is defined in very specific terms. Men are supposed to be controlling, dominant, decisive, and have all the answers. If and when you don't live up to any part of that definition, you are less of a man, and therefore less competent, less whole, less complete. "Being a man" happens to also correspond with being white, heterosexual, adult (but not old), upper-middle-class, able-bodied, and Protestant. If you don't live up to the image of "being a man" in any way, be that by choice or by birthright, then you are an "un-man," and a threat to patriarchy which must be silenced.

Most of us are taught from early on that hitting is wrong—"Don't hit your sister!" "Stop that, someone's going to get hurt." At the same time, we are taught to hit—"Protect yourself." "If someone messes with your sister, you clean his clock." "Violence" is frequently redefined depending on need. For example, in 1989 when the United States bombed Panama, the bombings were labeled "vertical insertion" as a way to hide the violence. This interesting choice of phraseology conjures up images that relate directly sexualized violence. This accommodation to violence is not new to military minds who recognize that, for most people, the use of violence is at times justified. Most people would argue that occasionally physical violence is justifiable. And even the Bible excuses the use of violence under certain circumstances. The vast majority of adults feel comfortable and justified in hitting children. In the end we are all left with attempting to determine for ourselves what is violence, and when the use of violence is acceptable and when it isn't.

For men, this training seems to be somewhat more disjointed. Men are supposed to be willing, prepared, and able to be brutally violent—to the point of killing up to thousands of people. We are taught that part of "being a man" is being willing and able to "protect" or "defend" "by any means necessary" whatever we may control: property, rights, justice, our country, or "our" women. At the same time, we're taught to not hit, to be patient and calm, and most recently to be "sensitive New Age guys." The mixed message inherent in this dual training establishes what can only be described as a mild form of societal schizophrenia. Men are taught that we aren't supposed to hit while at the same time being taught that to "be a man" we are supposed to be willing to go to war and kill for our country, or go to fisticuffs if the situation calls for it (such as our pride getting hurt, or some *thing* we own, like "our" women or "our" children getting damaged). As a result we aren't supposed to be violent, but defending yourself, protecting your honor, and punishing a child really isn't violence. Further, we come to understand that the definitions of "defending, protecting and punishing" may be determined by you in the moment.

This social, cultural, and personal pattern, that hides the truth and creates terms to describe violent actions without acknowledging the violence of the action, is very akin to the minimization and lying that is so prevalent in interpersonal violence. It creates a dynamic in which men's violence has become something very different: "It's not really violent . . . it was only a slap." "He was abused as a child; don't you understand?" "He was frustrated and doesn't know how to communicate." "He's an anti-sexist radical and it would be hypocritical for him to act like that." As we redefine violence according to our need, we effectively hide the truth. As I've discussed, we frequently describe violence using terms that deny the violence: it's "self-defense" or "punishment" or a "police action" or "vertical insertion." This same pattern appears with men who batter, who frequently claim that they "weren't violent, [they] were just trying to 'shut her up,' or get away." Likewise, men who rape (particularly those who haven't been convicted) frequently use other terms to refer to their behavior, and often exclaim that "she misunderstood" or that "[they] may have forced her but it wasn't really rape."

When the appropriate and truthful definition of the violence is expressed—rape, war, battering, abuse—and is expressed as *men's* violence, men feel justified (based on a system we have set up) in feeling blamed, or "misrepresented." When feminists label rape as men's violence, they are re-representing men's violence in response to its representation as "miscommunication" or "sex gone wrong." Whenever you directly confront commonly believed and socially sanctioned lies, it seems like a misrepresentation of the lie. It is, in fact, a re-representation—reclaiming the truth and re-becoming honest. As we've seen, men respond strongly to that re-representation. It's time we responded as strongly to the issues of rape, and other forms of men's violence, as we have to the re-representation.

Most of the time when violence is perpetrated it is perpetrated by men, regardless of the specific way it occurs: racist attacks, anti-Semitic bigotry, homophobic assaults, war, street violence, rape. This is not to say that men are wrong; it is meant to label the truth—*men perpetrate violence*. Men also do other things, and there is more to men than being perpetrators of violence, but the focus of this discussion is men's violence. Violence in whatever form is behavior that men choose, consciously or not, to perpetrate. Only men can make these behaviors come to an end.

All of us are exposed to patriarchal representations of men and men's violence on a continuous basis. Consequently, those of us who are men have internalized these messages and act them out. We doubt the statistics and the ways women describe the violence. We hold questions somewhere in our minds like "Is this really true?" "Was this really rape?" and "Why did she take her panty hose off?" We deny the extent of the effect on survivors lives: "Aren't you over it yet?!?"

Acting out the messages we learn from patriarchy, regardless of how "subtly" we may do so, effectively maintains and supports male domination. We, particularly men, effectively keep men in a position of supremacy over women via the personal interactions of our daily lives—thus, the personal is political. Patriarchy not only means a social, cultural and political system of oppression but also that individual men act out this oppression in our personal lives. Patriarchy would be nothing if it weren't for the individual men who bring the system to life. There are certainly the obvious examples—the men who attempt to deny women's reproductive options; the men who produce, distribute, and buy pornography; men who use sexist language; men who rape and men who batter, among others. But more subtle behaviors also maintain patriarchy: not confronting sexist language, interrupting women, accepting praise and fees for doing anti-rape educating, taking off our shirts when it's hot, walking alone on the streets at night wherever we choose, etc. Obviously, some of these behaviors are less hurtful than others, but they all support a larger system in which rape exists and flourishes. Referring to these behaviors as subtle is not necessarily an indication that they are somehow less oppressive than other behaviors, only that they are less frequently recognized as oppressive—particularly by those of us who behave in those manners. I am not saying that men who support patriarchy are "wrong" or "bad" (for all of us support patriarchy). However, it is important that we recognize the ways that we do support this system that dominates women as a class. Further, we need to begin challenging ourselves and each other about the ways that we do support male supremacy.

The intention behind our action doesn't matter. What matters is the outcome. Most men who batter don't "intend" to hurt their partner, don't "mean to" put their fist in her face. Many men who rape don't "mean to" rape. Regardless of the intention or the purpose, however, the outcome is what we must examine. It is our action's impact that we are accountable for. The outcome of men's behavior so far has been an exorbitant amount of violence, mostly directed at women, children, and other "un-men."

We are always on the lookout for an attractive person (female or male) whom we can objectify. I can hear your protestations from here: "Women do it too!" That may be true, to some extent, but that doesn't make it right, and we can't take responsibility for the behavior of women. We can only take responsibility for our own behaviors. I'm not saying that flirting or appreciating the beauty of someone's eyes is necessarily problematic, but rather that we need to deconstruct the process and look at *how* we flirt and *how* we appreciate his or her eyes. We have internalized patriarchal messages so effectively that we're always acting them out, and are rarely aware that we are doing that. In patriarchy, men "hunt" for a sexual partner; regardless of how subtly we act out that role, it is still abusive. One of the challenges in living an anti-rape lifestyle is to begin becoming aware of the ways you act out what you've learned in patriarchy.

Obviously this list of rape-supporting behaviors contains lots of contradictions. Does this mean that we don't take our shirts off when we're hot, or that we don't accept fees for doing an anti-rape training? Or do we stop going out on the streets at night? I can't answer these questions; there may not be any answer to these questions. The issue isn't that we don't support male supremacy in our actions—we will and we do. The issue is to begin becoming aware of the ways that we do, to take responsibility for our behavior, and to make some conscious choices about contradicting male supremacy. It isn't easy, but we need to make our minds large enough to handle the contradictions—for they are everywhere—particularly for men living anti-rape lifestyles.

Finally, the system of patriarchy works with the systems of white supremacy, heterosexual supremacy, class oppression, and adult supremacy. Furthermore, all of these systems, as they work together, are also brought to life in our personal relations: in the ways whites treat women and men of color; in the ways heterosexuals treat lesbians, gay men, and bisexuals; in the ways that adults treat children; and in the ways men treat women. The model is the same: Identify the differences, exploit those differences, slam those differences into a form of hierarchy in which men (or whites, or adults, or heterosexuals) are on top and start killing. It should be no shock to recognize this model as the one used by the military (ours as well that of other countries) to destroy the "enemy." It should quickly become apparent that women (and other un-men) are the "enemy" of patriarchy and, as such, must be destroyed.

## RAPE AS A WEAPON OF PATRIARCHY

Rape is one of the weapons used by the sociocultural/economic/ political system of patriarchy (and by individual men) to maintain men in a position of control and domination. Rape could not and does not happen in societies that are not built on male supremacy.* In her book *Surviving Sexual Violence*, Liz Kelly describes this clearly: "Power, inequality, and oppression function among socially constructed gender lines and, in this system, [male] violence is used to control women" (p.26). Rather than being the aberration that it is made out to be, rape is thus nothing more than an extension of normal male behavior. The politics that exist between women and men—the power differences and the ways that those power differences are played out—are a part of all of our interpersonal relationships. We cannot escape that, regardless of how hard we try. None of us have, as yet, progressed to the point of being able to relate with members of the so-called opposite sex without continuing to exemplify the wider world's system of male supremacy. Those of us who are male are inevitably privileged within these dynamics. The way we live our daily lives happens in a context—and that context is one of male supremacy. As such the ways we as men live our lives is made easier because of that context.

Oppression comes into play and continues to interfere with the ways we work, live, and play together. The sharpest example is that we, who happen to be male, have a choice of whether or not to live an anti-sexist lifestyle. We can always choose to stop. That isn't an option for women. Just surviving in this world means that they are choosing to live an anti-sexist lifestyle. It's very similar to lesbians, gay men, and bisexuals who, just by being alive, comfortable with themselves, and completely themselves (regardless of whether or not they are "out"), are a direct confrontation to heterosexism and heterosexual supremacy. Heterosexual people, on the other hand, have the option of whether or not to support queer liberation. So too it is for men. We can choose to live in direct contradiction of male supremacy, and we can choose how we enact that direct contradiction. We can choose to write a book against rape, but choose not to put the toilet seat down or share housework. We can choose

---

*Peggy Reeves Sanday, an anthropologist, most completely details this in her book *Female Power and Male Dominance: On the Origins of Sexual Inequality* (1981). Among other things, she found that in societies in which women and men had equal economic and political power rape was nonexistent, or extremely infrequent. Rape only occurred in societies in which there was mythical or real male dominance.

to become a member of NOW or the National Coalition Against Sexual Assault. We can choose to listen when someone with whom we are sharing sexually says no. Women have no such option. By definition, when they live their lives "out" as completely competent, empowered, complete, and fully human, they are in direct contradiction to how our culture says women should be.

These personal politics are only further complicated by other issues that frequently arise, such as race, class, sexual orientation, and age. The personal relationships that you and I have with women are tainted by male supremacy and the connected threat of rape. Male supremacy is part of our daily lives and, as such, is in our living rooms, our classrooms, our offices, and in our bedrooms. Rape culture makes it hard to communicate and truly listen to each other, interrupts our ability to be responsive and care for each other. In more ways than I can mention, rape culture is here, now.

## MEN'S CONFUSION: INTIMACY, SEX AND RAPE

Men and women tend to think about and experience sex differently and for different reasons. Additionally, the ways that women and men refer to and describe sex are different. Women tend to experience sex as an expression of or a building of intimate relationships. For most men, being intimate means being sexual, which requires a level of vulnerability. Sex is seen as *the* way that men can be intimate. For most women, being sexual is *a* way to be intimate, and being sexual is an expression of that intimacy, or a way to build towards greater intimacy.

Additionally, women and men frequently have conflicting motivations and expectations for physical and sexual intimacy. When those different expectations are separately acted upon without first being clarified, a conflict generally results. Men are taught to settle conflicts through the use of force in a wide variety of ways, including verbal pressure, physical intimidation, and emotional blackmail. When men use force against a date to settle a conflict about whether one person wants to be sexual and another doesn't, it becomes rape. Men rarely identify what they did as force, and therefore certainly not as rape. When you are taught from the earliest moments of life to use force to get your way—hit back, shoot to kill, be a little warrior, kill to defend your honor—then using emotional force to get sex doesn't compute as force. This should not be taken to mean that the man is any less responsible, or any less accountable, for his choices or behavior. It does, however, reinforce the need to listen to survivors when they say that they experienced force—or rape. It also reinforces the need for men to redefine force based on the definitions of people who have experienced being forced, as well as the need for men to deconstruct our understanding of force and the ways we express force.

Men are taught, from very early on, to not get or be intimate. However, intimacy—physical and emotional touching and closeness—is a basic human need. As human beings, we *must* share touch in order to survive! Most men only understand very limited kinds of intimacy—physical or sexual. This circumscription is clear when we watch men and physical closeness. Men either tackle each other on a football field, or have sex. Men rarely have physical contact at other times. And men seldom understand emotional or spiritual intimacy. As a result, and given that intimacy is a basic human need for all of us, men tend to feel a more desperate and intense need for intimacy. Our desire for intimacy, which we've confused with a desire for sex, can become so great as to overwhelm our partner—at which point it stops being sex and becomes rape. Regardless of how great our desire is, we are still in control of our behavior—and as such, are solely responsible for our actions.

Additionally, male culture objectifies women and depersonalizes sex. This is clearly exemplified in the language that is commonly used about men and sex: Men make love "to" our partners, men "score," or men "bust it out." This kind of language reinforces men as "actors," as the ones who act to or on women.

Traditionally, women respond to men's initiating behavior. Men make the first moves. In these kinds of relationships, men are in the power seat. It is that position of power and control that gets misused frequently and becomes rape. Rape needs this kind of power imbalance and these kinds of dynamics to occur.

Men's desire for sex, and the desire for control of the relationship, can and frequently does get confusing. We live in a culture in which power and control have become eroticized. Being "in control" is a sexual rush for men. There is a sexual high that comes from being "powerful." We hear it talked about all the time—the "seductiveness" of power—"She looks so good I could rape her here and now," someone says. Much of our advertising clearly exemplifies, through a variety of means, a power difference that is exploited and sexualized. Because, in part, of this eroticization of power, it is difficult to distinguish (even for men) whether a man is "getting off" on the force, on sharing sex, or on being intimate with somebody. When a man forces a women or other man to be sexual when she or he doesn't want to, it can be more from a desire for control than a desire for sex.

## RAPE AND RACISM

Male supremacy and white supremacy work in concert. These two political, economic, legal, and educational systems interlock to maintain white men in positions of domination over white women as well as over women and men of color. A part of this domination has become sexualized. Lies have been created and are maintained of the "Black male rapist" along with the "Black woman seductress." Angela Davis, in her monumental work *The Myth of the Black Rapist*, clearly exposes these lies, tracing their origins in slavery. While Davis focuses on Black men and women, I would argue that this dynamic works similarly for all men and women of color: Hispanic, Native American, Asian, and Middle Eastern. The specific dynamics are different from one racial group to another, but the underlying patterns are the same. Davis reminds us:

> Slavery relied as much on routine sexual abuse as it relied on the whip and the lash. Excessive sexual urges, whether they existed among individual white men or not, had nothing to do with this virtual institutionalization of rape. Sexual coercion was an essential dimension of the social relations between slavemaster and slave. In other words, the right claimed by slaveowners and their agents over the bodies of female slaves was a direct expression of their presumed property rights of Black people as a whole. The license to rape aminated from and facilitated the ruthless economic domination that was the gruesome hallmark of slavery (p.179).

The term "myth" is frequently used, as I've done above, to describe these dynamics. Using that word, however, effectively minimizes the damage created as a result of these lies. Myths are simple, they are rather playful, and they are generally not particularly hurtful. "Myths" conjures up images of dragons and damsels in distress. These lies of the man of color rapist tied with the lies of the woman of color seductress were just that—*lies*. They were consciously created, and viciously enforced. They resulted in the violent deaths of countless men and women of color by white men. Furthermore, when Black men and women were lynched, they were often sexually abused during the lynching.

To believe that European American men's sexual abuse of Black women and violence against Black men through fabricated charges of rape stopped when slavery stopped is to deny historical reality and to conveniently put our heads in the sand. Not only did it continue (and increase during several periods), but it is still going on. For example, few of us have forgotten the brutal attack of the white woman in Central Park by a gang of Black youth in 1988. This was in fact a horrible, brutal, vicious attack. It also received a great amount of national press coverage. Not two days after this attack however, a Black woman was similarly attacked by a gang of white youth and thrown out of a seventh-story window. That story received no national attention, and precious little public outcry. This discrepancy in outrage and publicity simultaneously sends—and exposes—a powerful message about the value we place on the lives of women of color and white women.

European American men have benefited from these lies in a number of ways. We who are white are able to have access to a larger number of women for our sexual and violent exploitation, while minimizing the "competition" (note the inherent competition mindset that is part of patriarchal thinking). At the same time, we maintain our position of being the "hero on the white horse" for "our" women who are then put into an increasingly vulnerable position. And as we have come to know, it is just those women—the women for whom we are the "hero"—that we are most likely to victimize.

In order to work effectively against rape, we *must* work also against racism. Even when we don't do anti-racist work directly, it is essential that we make clear that doing anti-rape work is connected to do anti-racist work. Rape happens not only in a context of male supremacy but also in a context of white supremacy. Furthermore, the use and maintenance of this lie effectively maintains a wedge between the political alliance of people of color and white women. By keeping that alliance from becoming fully established, white men maintain positions of domination.

## HETEROSEXISM AND SEXUAL ASSAULT

We also find a clear connection between heterosexism (the presumption of the inherent superiority of heterosexuals and the hatred of homosexuality and gay, lesbian, and bisexual people) and sexual assault. (I will use the term "gay people" to refer to gay, lesbian, and bisexual people). Gay people have been sexually victimized by heterosexuals to punish them for their sexual orientation. Gay and bisexual men are not infrequently sexually victimized during hate attacks (which have been increasing since statistics have been kept by the National Gay and Lesbian Task Force Anti-Violence Project). Likewise, lesbians and bisexual women have been sexually harassed and sexually assaulted because they were "out" as lesbian or bi women.

Furthermore, lesbian and gay baiting has been used against women and men who have spoken out against sexism and sexual violence. It is common for women who describe themselves as feminists to be labeled as lesbian—as if there is something wrong with that—in an attempt to silence or shame them into silence and submission. And they are often harassed if they do identify as lesbian.

Additionally, heterosexuals have created lies about the threat that gay people pose to children. We all know this lie: that gay people "recruit" children. If we dissect this, it is really a concern (based on mis- and disinformation) that gay people sexually abuse children at a greater rate than heterosexual people. This vicious lie has absolutely no basis in what we know, and the evidence shows, to be true. The vast majority of men who sexually abuse children are heterosexual men—whether they abuse girls or boys. This is not to say that there aren't gay men who abuse children, but the real threat to children is heterosexual men. Like the lies/myths of rape and racism, these lies have been created and are maintained to enforce systemic domination over gay and bisexual people. These lies, and the fear they fuel, are used by heterosexist culture to continue to deny homosexual and bisexual people the same rights that heterosexual people have: the right to be openly in love and to express their love in public, the right to be a foster parent or a "big brother" or "big sister," the right to have their life partner covered by their employer's health insurance, and more. As we have already discussed, rather than being an increased risk as sexual victimizers, gay people are actually at increased risk for being sexually victimized.

Finally, heterosexism is used to keep people aligned with their socially defined gender roles: being a "man" or being a "woman." How many of us, as we grew up, were taunted with acting "like a girl" or "being a wuss" or some other term that called our attention to how we didn't quite live up to the ideals of what "being a man" is? How many women were baited by taunts of lesbianism or "trying to be a man" when they stepped out of the culturally defined ways that a woman should act? The fear of being queer is enough to keep most of us acting just as we should in relation to our gender roles.

## THE ROLE OF PORNOGRAPHY*

Any discussion of rape culture that doesn't also examine the connection of pornography is incomplete—it would reinforce that very rape culture in the way that any silence about oppression reinforces that oppression. To fully understand rape in our society requires an understanding of pornography.

---

*Thanks to Daryl Spears for his assistance and support in developing this section.

The pornography industry is a huge industry. There are more pornography shops in this country than McDonald's. Pornography brings in more money than the music and movie industries combined. And, while speaking in Europe in 1992, I learned that the United States is the largest exporter of pornography, and the largest importer of women and children for the sex slave trade. It seems beyond dispute that a clear connection exists between pornography and sexual violence.

Traditional legal definitions of pornography have focused on pornography as expression, rather than on pornography as real harm caused to real women. As Andrea Dworkin and Catherine MacKinnon wrote in *Pornography and Civil Rights: A New Day for Women's Equality*, "Instead of recognizing the personal injuries and systematic harms of pornography, the law has told the society that pornography is a passive reflection or one-level-removed 'representation' or symptomatic by-product or artifact of the real world" (p.26). As a result, the damage done by pornography is kept hidden, and the focus of the argument stays misplaced on "freedom of speech" and "freedom of expression," without any discussion of whose freedom, or of the responsibility for our speech.

I take my definition of pornography, for the purposes of this book, from the Minneapolis City Ordinance on Pornography, which was cowritten by MacKinnon and Dworkin. (Similar ordinances have been filed in Massachusetts, Indianapolis, and Cambridge.) Pornography, therefore, is here defined as "a form of discrimination on the basis of sex. Pornography is the sexually explicit subordination of women, graphically depicted, whether in pictures or in words..." (*Pornography and Civil Rights*, p.101)

The way that women are portrayed in pornography is overwhelmingly constructed and engineered by male photographers, male producers, and male writers for the sexual pleasure of male audiences. Those women are depicted with no personality, and no depth. They are incomplete; we can see that in the pictures and the writing of pornography. The images have no substance—they are purely the embodiment of a pleasure tool for men.

For most men, using pornography is our first sexual experience. This sexual experience is based on an "interaction" with a two-dimensional, man-made image of what a woman is or should be. The point is that this "interaction" is really no interaction at all; it is noncommunicative, one-way, purely physical sensation with no emotional feeling attached. As Daryl Spears argues:

> Pornography for men, then, is something more than an issue of the depiction of sexual acts. It is structurally built into the maintenance of a sense of identity that pivots on the extent of their closeness to the

"essence of man." The use of pornography as a creator of the terms of
that eroticized difference (Daryl Spears, forthcoming).

This early training for most of us teaches that sexual involvement is
about our sexual satisfaction with no emotional "entanglement." If she gets
satisfied, that's fine—it's even great. But the focus of any sexual
interaction is our satisfaction. Our orgasm marks the end of any sexual
engagement—not hers.

Pornography teaches men how to be sexual with "women," as they are
defined in pornography, which is reinforced in the larger culture. "Here's
how to act out male supremacy in sex. Here are the acts that impose
power over and against another body," is how John Stoltenberg so
eloquently describes it. *That* is the central theme of pornography. That is
also the central theme of rape. This training happens in a context, as I've
described, in which well over half of all women are sexually
victimized—mostly by the men in their lives. A context that is inherently
political. And a context to which you, I, and all of us have a personal stake.

Given that pornography is generally men's first sexual experience, what
impact does that have when we begin having two-way sexual encounters
with multi-dimensional, emotional, very real human beings? How do these
experiences reinforce the notion of men pushing for sexual encounters?
The answers to these question are, as yet, still unclear. However, given
that most human behavior is based, in part, on our experiences in the past,
it seems safe to assume that the way we share sex with people is at least
in part based on this early training.

Pornography is pro-rape propaganda. It depicts the actual or simulated
victimization, dehumanization, and violation of women as somehow
"sexy." The basic tenets of pornography include the degradation of
woman, the sex act as all physical sensation and no emotion, and men as
perpetrators. As Andrea Dworkin so clearly reminds us, "Male power is
the raison d'etre of pornography, the degradation of the female is the
means of achieving this power." The women within pornography are
displayed as enjoying and deserving the exploitation—which sets up a
mindset, and reinforces a culture, that sees the exploitation of women as
not particularly harmful. As tragic as this, is men who view pornography
tend to view women in general in the same light as the women are
portrayed in pornography. We look to all women as perhaps being women
of the pornographic principle, women who live up to the image that was
portrayed in the magazine or video last night. The woman loses her
individual autonomy and integrity, and is measured against the airbrushed
fictional character on a screen.

Pornography is the depiction of the theme "man fucks woman" (Catherine MacKinnon first depicted this dynamic). When we break down that sentence into its grammatical parts, we get: man (subject, actor, center of the world) fucks (violent verb) woman (object on which the actor does the verb). We don't know the "true" incidence of sexual abuse of women in pornography, but there is a clear connection. It has been demonstrated that a majority of the women in pornography are survivors of sexual abuse as children—an experience that concretely reinforces the notion that their value as a human being is based on their physical attractiveness and their willingness to be sexually pleasing and available to men.

Furthermore, these depictions are also full of very racist, anti-Semitic, and homophobic overtones. When "lesbian" scenes are displayed, they are depicted as the male fantasy would have lesbian scenes—for the pleasure of the man. They are not a depiction of an encounter between two women who wish to sexually please themselves and each other.

Within pornography, the depictions of beauty, of the "sexual," and of power are white-based within pornography, as they are in the rest of our culture. When women of color are depicted in pornography, they are depicted basically as being dark-skinned white women (women of color who have very Caucasoid features). Women of color and Jewish women are much more likely to be depicted tied up, brutalized, and shown with more than one male participant and/or with animals than are white women. This truth further fuels the racist rape attitudes that we as white men were raised with of the "women of color seductress" (described above). What happens when these depictions are put out into a culture where white supremacy reigns, and where the history of white male sexual violence against women and men of color is long and brutal?

There is an ongoing, vehement debate about so-called hard- versus soft-core pornography, and the attempts to make a distinction between pornography and "erotica." The difference between the two was created by the law to distinguish between pornography that displayed an erect penis (hard core) and that which did not (soft core). As the pornography industry has developed, a blurring between these has occurred. Socially, the distinction seems to be that which is acceptable, and that which pushes the boundaries of "good taste." This truly is a false distinction. So-called soft-core pornography, mostly understood as *Playboy* and *Penthouse*, simply works to mainstream the sexual exploitation of women. Of course, women are exploited and sexualized in other forms of media as well: MTV, most R-rated movies (particularly those targeting teenage audiences), the majority of advertising, etc. This doesn't mean that pornography is not harmful, but rather that these expressions of women-hate are tolerated by the mainstream.

While some differences do exist, these differences are more a matter of degree than substance. Because we have all grown and developed in *this* context, which is both woman hating and sex-phobic (the irrational fear of sex), we all have some degree of both in us. Frankly, none of us know how to create sexually explicit materials that aren't objectifying. Further, the so-called soft-core pornography or "erotica" is generally as racist, anti-Semitic, and generally heterosexist as is the hard-core pornography. For those of you who still question the importance of understanding pornography, try to image a rape-free world that maintains and supports pornography.

## CONTINUUM OF RAPE/SEXISM

It is in men's interest, as the perpetrators of sexual violence, that definitions of forms of sexual violence be as limited as possible. At the same time, women [and women survivors] are unable to name their abuse as abuse, men are able to deny responsibility for abusive behavior. Language is a further means of controlling women. Defining sexual violence in terms of a continuum...provides women [and women survivors] with a means of defining their specific experience as abuse (Kelly, pp. 156-57).

Contrary to popular belief, rape and other forms of men's violence occur on a continuum of behavior. On one end of the continuum exists "normal" everyday male behavior, attitudes, and beliefs. On the other end, extreme forms of oppression, degradation, and violence. Along the continuum lie the so-called normal and, certainly, the everyday expressions of sexism and male privilege. For example, somewhere along the continuum are behaviors such as using exclusive, sexist language, or describing women as objects or as otherwise in-human. We act out expressions of sexism and male supremacy in countless ways that we often are not completely, or often even partially, aware of. One of the ways that we can begin to work against rape is to identify our own expressions of sexism and the ways that we act along the continuum—and interrupt those behaviors.

A major piece of what keeps this continuum as a continuum, and keeps it alive and well, is its underlying attitudes and beliefs. The behaviors are only part of the problem, since dissecting the underlying rape-supporting attitudes that keep sexism in place is also essential to stopping rape. When we express these behaviors or the underlying attitudes, regardless of how subtle or overt those behaviors may be, we support the system—this continuum—that accepts, allows, and even encourages rape and more extreme forms of men's violence. Furthermore, we act as reminders to women that we are in touch with that power—a power that we can choose whether or not to take to its extreme of rape.

The continuum that follows is based on the work of Liz Kelly, who eloquently describes the rape continuum in her book *Surviving Sexual Violence* (pp.76-94).

Continuum of Behaviors:

  ° mutual sexual interrelationships

  ° men controlling touch between intimates

  ° men controlling sexual interactions

  ° men expecting to share sex with someone and acting on that assumption without first asking

  ° referring to women as "bitches"

  ° buying/viewing pornography

  ° men limiting women's choices

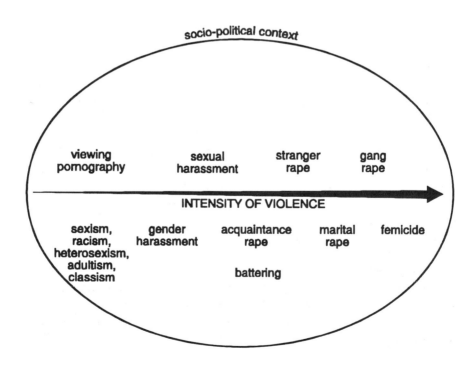

⁰ men not listening when s/he says no

⁰ men walking down the street and whistling at women

⁰ men pressuring or manipulating their partners to have sex

⁰ men using force to have sex

⁰ violent gang rape resulting in death of the victim

A second view of the continuum of sexism may help to clarify the connections in other ways. This is a continuum that clearly delineates the issues of sexism and how they are interrelated. It is important to note that this continuum does not exist on a hierarchy, and that all of these behaviors support the other behaviors on the continuum. It is also important to examine the other supporting structures of this continuum, since sexism doesn't work alone. Racism, homophobia, adultism, classism, and able-ism all work along with sexism to maintain rape culture. This truth has been clearly exposed by a number of theorists and activists (among them bell hooks, Elias Farajaja-Jones, Gloria Anzaldua, and Angela Davis). And it is no better exemplified than in the situation of sexual violence.

What keeps these behaviors connected is that they all work to oppress women—in different ways. Furthermore, people who experience these behaviors often report very similar feelings, so although the intensity of the feelings may increase as one proceeds along the continuum, the feelings themselves are strikingly similar. Finally, all of these behaviors are supported by the same underlying attitudes and assumptions. To effectively eradicate these behaviors, we need to begin identifying, labeling, and challenging the underlying attitudes from which these behaviors grow.

It is also important to point out that the levels of physical violence increase as one proceeds along the continuum.

This continuum isn't a completely accurate description in that the existence of these forms of violence are not necessarily linear. Furthermore, many of the behaviors that I described are also attitudes that support some of the other behaviors. However, this does offer a view of the ways that all forms of sexism are interrelated and depicts the need to confront the more subtle forms of sexism and oppression in order to eliminate rape.

Men frequently argue that there is a difference between the way that we share sex with the people we are intimate with and rape, and that it is unfair to put all sexual interactions on the same plane as sexual violence. However, all of us have used various forms of pressure, force, and manipulation and coercion to get what we want—to share sexually. All of us have had times when we have been with someone who didn't want to share sex with us, and who was quite clear about that, and we kept pressuring or kept trying. We all have examples of times when the person we were sharing sex with said no, and we listened to that for a time, but at some point tried again, and again, and again. Because of the content in which our interpersonal sexual relations occur, few if any of us know what a truly mutual relationship looks like. Because male supremacy is so insidious in our lives, all of us act out subtle (and not so subtle) expressions of it in our personal relationships.

It is interesting to dissect men's sexual activity in this light. Frequently in the early stages of a sexual relationship, men are planning how to move towards sex. We start kissing and a frequent early thought is when to make a move towards caressing her breast or touching his chest. Depending on the reaction of the person we are with, we'll begin thinking towards the next step. If our hand is moved away, we tend to begin thinking of when to try again. It's a very common pattern. This is not a picture of equality and mutuality. This is a picture of coercion. No, it's not rape, but it does exist in the same mindset.

THREE

# WHY MEN RAPE

THOUSANDS OF THEORIES are floating around about why men rape. In fact, there seem to be almost as many theories as there are men who rape. This chapter is not meant as a definitive discussion of those theories. Rather, I will focus on two as a point of departure: the work of psychologist Nicholas Groth, and that of sociologist Diane Scully—both of whom base their analyses on their work with men in prison who have been convicted of rape. From there, I examine the various cultural underpinnings that create rape as an option for men.

Frequently, men who rape, and the women and men who survive sexual assault, describe the attack so differently as to lead one to believe they were, in fact, completely different situations. However, the definition must rely on the interpretation of the survivor. That person and that person alone best knows if what occurred went beyond his or her limits, and whether or not what happened was rape. That person and that person alone knows if she or he was or felt forced to do something sexual that she or he didn't want to or wasn't prepared for. If someone reports feelings of anger, powerlessness, confusion, relief, pain, shame, or sadness in relation to a sexual encounter of some kind, then it is likely that person experienced some form of sexual violence—even if those exact words aren't used to describe his or her experience.

For years feminists have attempted to shatter the view that men rape to satisfy a need for sexual gratification. Despite the work that has been done, and the frequent lip service that our society gives to understanding rape as a violent act, there continues to be a strong assumption that men rape out of sexual frustration, desire, or an "overwhelming need" for sexual gratification. For example, we frequently hear questions such as "What was she wearing?" or "What was she doing out that late anyway?" These kinds questions are not only survivor-blaming, since women have the right to wear anything they choose without fear of attack, but also attempt to link rape with the "sexual provocativeness" of the woman who was raped.

Another example of this same kind of thinking is the frequently intense arguments with men around the issue of respecting women when they say no, every time they say no, regardless of how or when they say no. Men frequently attempt to give examples of women who have said no and "didn't really mean it." This reasoning is not only thinly veiled survivor-blaming but is also an attempt to allude to men's and women's supposedly unclear thinking when "overcome with passion."

At some level, men also understand that rape is a violent act. As one young man said during a college presentation I offered, "I agree that rape is a violent act, but how do you know when it is really rape?" There are several parts to that seemingly simple question. One piece of that question is plain ignorance. Part of that question is an attempt to undermine the very understanding he claimed to have of rape as a violent act ("It's really confusing—you're making out and getting all excited and she seems to be enjoying it—how do you know it's "really" what she claims it was?"). Part of that question comes from wanting to see himself as different from "those men" who rape ("How do I know that what I did last week isn't rape?"). Part of that question is an attempt to understand why men perpetrate violent acts on the person we claim to care for.

Most men who rape do not identify what they did as rape. Generally, men who rape—particularly men who have perpetrated acquaintance rape—describe their behavior in any number of other ways that distinguish what they did from anything that could be construed as rape. For example, rape has been described as consensual sex where women "changed their minds." Men tend to think of what we do with women—particularly on dates—as being within the bounds of what is expected. We are supposed to "push the limits" with our date. We are expected, and expect ourselves, to "get as far as we can" in "trying to score." We usually feel entitled to at least a hug, if not a kiss and then some, when we go on a date. After all, "isn't that the purpose of a date?" "So perhaps he got a little out of hand in trying to get a kiss; it certainly wasn't rape!"

Men identified as rapists are generally portrayed as some kind of monster. Men certainly don't want to see ourselves or the men we know as a "monster," and so go through all kinds of mental gymnastics to distance ourselves from "those" men. When the man who is accused of rape is seen as "the boy next door," then the conversation immediately turns to examining the woman's motivations for "trying to bring this poor guy down." However, the basic questions remain unanswered: Why do men, any men, rape?

While men rape for a variety of reasons, most often it is motivated by a desire for power, control, and domination. Nicholas Groth is a psychologist and researcher on rape issues who for the past twenty years has worked with men in prison who rape. He has created a paradigm to describe possible motivations for men raping, which outlines three types of rape behavior. It should be emphasized that these are rather arbitrary distinctions and are not either-or categories—they are fluid, and sometimes men will rape within what looks like one category, and rape a second time within what looks like another category. Moreover, at times rape may overlap categories. Distinguishing these categories helps for simplicity's sake in sharing this information, but it should not be taken as hard and fast rules about human behavior—even raping behavior.

According to Nicholas Groth:

∘ The Power Rapist is the most common form of rapist, accounting for approximately 95 percent of all rapists. The men who "power rape" rape to gain a sense of power out of the rape attack. They want to feel "in control" and use the rape attack as a way of meeting that need. Rarely is the rape victim/survivor injured during a "power rape."

∘ The Anger Rapist is the second most frequent kind of rapist and accounts for approximately 4 percent of all rapists. The men who "anger rape" rape as a way of releasing angry feelings they have. Generally it will result in some physical injury to the victim/survivor.

∘ The Sadist Rapist is the rarest form of rapist, accounting for less than 1 percent of all rapes. Due to the titillating nature of these attacks, these are the most frequently publicized rapes. An example of this kind of rape is the Jeffrey Dahmer case of the spring of 1991. Men who "sadistically rape" (i.e. rape *and* want to physically damage the person they are raping) will often "get off" on the fact that they are hurting the person they are raping. This form of rape will generally result in severe physical injury or the death of the victim/survivor (Groth, pp.171).

Dr. Groth worked with men in prison; this fact shapes his work, and several caveats must be offered before we take his analysis into the broader population. Firstly, men in prison for rape are overwhelmingly sentenced for stranger rape. Although some dynamics may be similar to acquaintance rape, there are also a number of differences that have yet to be fully explored. One difference is that when a relationship does exist, physical violence and intimidation is less likely and less frequent. We know, for example, that stranger rape is characterized by higher amounts of physical violence and the use of weapons. Emotional manipulation and more subtle uses of control appear to be truer with acquaintance rape. Furthermore, survivors of acquaintance rape appear to have a stronger motivation for not hurting the man who rapes them than is true with stranger rape.

Additionally, a difficulty in with working with men in prison is that it is often a biased population. As is true regardless of their crime, men in prison are more frequently poor and working-class men, and men of color. This isn't to say that men of color or poor and working-class men aren't necessarily representative of white men and more wealthy men in the case of rape. It is to acknowledge that the legal system of this country is racist and classist and that bias will impact any attempts to understand criminal behavior based on looking at men in prison.

In acquaintance rape situations, which make up the vast majority of rapes, it appears that men rape as a result of feelings of entitlement. To follow through by using Groth's paradigm, either power or anger would appear as the primary motivation—power in relation to having the entitlement in the first place (being "entitled" represents a "power over" position), and anger for being kept from what he feels he is entitled to. Men tend to assume, for any number of reasons, that we are entitled to have our sexual desires met, that men are entitled to share sexually with people we are attracted to, and that we are entitled to a "payback" for taking someone out. This sense of entitlement seems to be reinforced when we become sexually aroused: "We are entitled to sexual release, which is the responsibility of the person we are out with—the person who got us sexually aroused in the first place." This feeling of entitlement can be based on any number of reasons, including

- if he pays
- if he drives
- if they have been sexual with each other previously
- if he gets sexually excited
- if he thinks that sex is on the agenda
- what she wears

When what men desire is not forthcoming (i.e., when his partner is unwilling to have sex) most men respond by attempting to "take it"—directly, manipulatively, or suggestively. "We have a right to what we want and one way or another, we're going to get it." This is part of where the line between "those" men who rape and the rest of us begins to blur. In order to be "real men," we are supposed to see what we want, and get it, almost at any cost. That is what being masculine is supposedly about, that is part of what makes us "sexy." It is just that kind of thinking, in the "right" situation, that leads to sexual assault.

Just this kind of reasoning is what needs to be countered to end men's violence. It is *never* acceptable to force another person to be sexual. Additionally, and more basically, these underlying attitudes of entitlement must be challenged. We need to deconstruct why we are "supposed" to get sexual release every time we become aroused. Where do these beliefs come from? Why is it the responsibility of my date to meet those needs? These basic questions, which lead us back to traditional masculinity, are the questions that we as men need to examine in a context of working and living to stop rape. We need to examine, man-to-man, why we think we should "get what we want when we want it," and why that applies to other human beings.

Feminists have raised some concerns with the paradigm set forth by Groth. Most of these concerns center upon the tendency to use this paradigm as a way of not holding men accountable or responsible for their behavior. By suggesting that men who rape are driven by "power, anger, or sadism," it has been argued, Groth is taking rape out of the realm of personal choices by men who rape, and into the arena of psychotherapy—which tends to depoliticize issues such as sexual violence. Further, the paradigm fails to examine why sex has gotten tangled with notions of power, anger, and sadism for most if not all men. That lack, inadvertently, reinforces the idea that rape is perpetrated by "those" men who are somehow different than I am.

Diane Scully, in her book *Understanding Sexual Violence: A Study of Convicted Rapists* (1990), concluded that men who are sentenced for rape are virtually no different than men on the street. She noted that convicted rapists show no increased signs of sociological or pathological impairment. Based on her research:

- 50 percent of rapists report growing up in nonabusive families,

- 66 percent said that they had not been physically abused as children, and

- 91 percent denied experiencing childhood sexual abuse.

In terms of their relationships with women, Scully found that they tended to have slightly more relationships than other men, and often described their significant relationships in positive terms. They describe themselves as having had "ample sexual opportunities" and relationships with women that were not at all uncommon compared to those of their peers. According to Scully, "both sexual frustration/deprivation and sexual psychopathology lack utility as general explanations for rape."

Rather than being "abnormal" in some (or any) way, Scully found that the convicted rapists she interviewed were very "normal." If anything, they were "hyper-normal," meaning that they identified strongly with the ideas and ideals of traditional masculinity. Their views about women and femininity largely reflected the most romanticized ideas of mainstream culture: women were seen as on a pedestal, as deserving to be revered, and more virtuous than men. Similarly, their ideas about masculinity were based on the very central themes found in mainstream culture: men as action and achievement oriented, dominant, levelheaded, daring and aggressive, constantly ready for sex. As such, the difference between men who are caught for rape and the rest of us is more a matter of degree than substance. Remember the continuum of sexism discussed in chapter 2, and the very strong correlation can be seen.

The primary reason, I would argue, that men are sexually violent is because we choose to be, and because we can be. All forms of sexual violence, regardless of the amount of planning or not, are choices that men make. They are choices that men can choose not to make. Rape is not an "uncontrollable urge" that comes over a man as he walks down a street, watches a woman, or gets sexually aroused. Rape is a behavior that is chosen.

Behaviors result from decisions. That may seem so basic to not need to be stated, but sometimes it is important to state the obvious. People generally choose how they act. Their choices may not be conscious, but they are choices nonetheless, and we can make our choices conscious. And regardless of whether choices are conscious, they are still our choices, and we are still responsible. For example, if you were to think right now about the last decision you made, you would probably consider deciding what to wear today, or deciding to read this book right now as opposed to watching TV or calling a friend. However, choosing to respond to these questions and think about what your last decisions were are also choices. What you're doing with your hands, your feet, the way that you are breathing are all choices that can become conscious.

This issue of choice relates to rape because many men who rape don't identify their behavior as sexually abusive. We may not necessarily choose to rape, but we do choose to not listen when the person we are with says no (regardless of how that person may say no); we choose not to ask before we touch a friend in a sexual or sensual way; we choose to hold her head when we kiss her (you know, that "romantic" kiss where she can't turn away). Those kinds of behaviors are chosen by the person who acts them out. Those kinds of behaviors can also be abusive. We need to take responsibility for our actions, our behaviors, our choices, and the consequences of those choices. When men rape, men are making a decision. Again, we may not be aware of the decision we are making, but it is a decision, a choice, nonetheless. *And* we are responsible and accountable for those choices.

## DATING RULES/DATING ROLES

It isn't very often talked about, and is rarely made conscious, but we all seem to know that there are specific rules and roles that go along with dating. On some basic level we intuit what these roles and rules are, or, at least, that there are "rules to date by." Because the model of dating and coupling is heterosexually based, and because of heterosexism, most of what we assume to be true about dating roles is based on the patterns of men and women. Typically, one takes on the role of nurturer or care-taker, one takes the role of decision-maker; one takes role of initiator (the one who calls, who initiates touching, etc.), the other is the responder, etc. In most heterosexual relationships, the male takes on the role of the decision-maker and initiator, and the female becomes the nurturer/care-taker and responder. His role is to set up the date, decide where they are going when and how, and to initiate any physical and/or sexual encounter. Her responsibility is to respond to his advances and/or to set limits. Given that her responsibility is often also to please him, it becomes easy for him to manipulate her into a potentially uncomfortable position.

Unfortunately, two people often have very different ideas about what the rules are and how the roles get played out in specific situations. It is important to be clear that all of us have the ability to fill these and any other roles in our intimate relationships. We need to talk with each other throughout the dating process to clarify the roles we are playing, the rules we are playing by, if we are comfortable in those roles, and any expectations that may arise. There is nothing wrong with having expectations; we all do. The problem, and potential rape, is when we begin acting out those expectations without first checking them out with the person we are acting our expectations out upon.

The ways that heterosexism impacts acquaintance rape in same-sex relationships is unclear. Gay and bisexual people live in an environment in which their love and the expression of their love is not only illegal but can bring a violent response—up to and including being killed. The impact that living and trying to love in that kind of context has on the dating roles and rules certainly changes the landscape in ways that are immeasurable. The situation also creates an environment where acquaintance rape is not discussed. Survivors don't come out, victimizers aren't held accountable, and the issues remain undiscussed. It's a terrible bind. To acknowledge that same-sex acquaintence rape happens adds fuel to a viciously heterosexist culture that is seemingly tireless in its efforts to squash and destroy gay and bi culture and people. To not acknowledge it leaves gay and bi survivors in the lurch—they don't receive appropriate services by the survivor-service community, and they don't receive adequate support by the gay and bi communities. For those of you who are heterosexual, you have the responsibility to take on and eliminate the heterosexism of the culture.

## THE LESSONS OF WAR AND PEACE

We live in a militaristic culture. Our country was founded on conquest and militarism, our economy is fueled primarily by the military, and many of our leaders come from military backgrounds. In a number of ways, the military has infected our daily lives. This is particularly true for men. From very early on, men are trained to be prepared for war. We're taught to hit and to take a punch. We have it ingrained in us that men are soldiers, men shoot, men kill. We are told that to "be a man" we must register for the draft and, beginning very young, are taught to be aware of and prepared for the possibility of killing people. Additionally, many of the skills (or lack thereof) men have in resolving conflicts are lessons learned in the military or as as a result of living in a militaristic culture. However disgusting it may be to us personally, we learn how to think like a soldier.

During wartime, women and children are traditionally considered the unofficial (and frequently the official) "spoils of war." The rape of women by soldiers during a war has a long and deep tradition in any military. It is considered one of the methods of demoralizing the "enemy." Sexual atrocities have been reported recently as perpetrated by Serbian soldiers against Bosnian Muslim women and children. Reports indicate that the violence is being sanctioned by the military high command as a way to defeat the Bosnian resistance. Other examples, among countless others, include the systematic rape of Vietnamese women by U.S. soldiers, the rape of Jewish women by German soldiers, the rape of Confederate women by Union soldiers (and vice versa).

Women and children are often victimized and killed by war and the male soldiers as much as, if not more than, male soldiers. Victimizing the women and children of the "enemy" is seen as a part of war. Men's violence against women and children is viewed as one of the side effects (once in a while, we'll even hear it described as one of the "negative" side effects) of war. Describing it as a "side effect" effectively places rape on a back burner to be responded to at some point. We're still waiting. Further, by painting the pain and victimization of women and children as a "side effect," the military can get away without recognizing these "casualties" and with dismissing them outright.

Women have also been set up as the "entertainment" for male warriors. (Note that I stated "women" are the entertainment. It isn't women's skills or talent that is the entertainment, it is women themselves.) And this "entertainment" is frequently based on the further victimization and violation of women by men—it only takes different forms. Much of this "entertainment" is officially sanctioned and established by the U.S. government, as in the sex industry that is often deliberately created around U.S. military bases. This dynamic again points up the relationship of sexism, racism, classism, and adultism since it is generally young women and children from poor and working class backgrounds who are most frequently employed by the sexploitation industry which is established around military bases. It is usually women and some men of color who are enticed into the pay-for-sex businesses.

Since we tend to attack nations of color that are already economically exploited (such as Vietnam, Korea, the Philippines, and Iraq), we put added pressure on these economies, which are already struggling to meet the needs of their people. When our (male) soldiers go to those countries with money to spend, it adds another level of pressure on women and children because the sexploitation industry is an opportunity for them to bring in some desperately needed money for their families. As such, their participation in sex slavery becomes less and less a "choice" and more a necessity for survival!

As if this weren't bad enough, the physical, psychological, social, or spiritual injuries that women and children receive as a result of war are rarely attended to by the services which are established and offered to soldiers. As countries divert ever-increasing resources to the war effort, fewer resources remain to provide services for civilian victims of war. Further, as more resources are spent on the war, an increase results in the victimizing that occurs in relation to that war. As a result of these various forms of men's victimizing behaviors, women and children are frequently ravaged during wartime.

These lessons, like so many others from the military, are an integral part of our daily lives, and are entrenched in our culture during so-called peacetime. Perhaps the military itself has offered us the most clear examples of this. In the spring of 1992, there was an incident known as the Tailhook scandal, during which naval officers and enlisted men, at a private hotel, forced female soldiers as well as female civilians through a gauntlet in which the women were verbally harassed, pawed, physically attacked, groped, had their clothes ripped off, and were otherwise sexually attacked. The initial Navy response minimized it, describing it as understandable within the military mindset. It was only after outside pressure was put on the Navy that it began to respond more appropriately. Another example is the old Marine Corps chant:

> This is my weapon
> This is my gun (point to groin)
> This one's for killing
> This one's for fun.

This slogan clearly demonstrates, socializes, and condones the mindset of "penis as weapon."

Military training uses men's learned hatred of femininity (and by association, of women as a class) to motivate men to be killing machines. Military training reinforces in brutal ways the understanding of femininity as synonymous with weakness. In order to be "men," "weakness" must be eliminated. Young soldiers-to-be are frequently taunted during training as "women," "nothing but a bunch of little girls," and "wusses." In the process, they are taught to hate anything having to do with femininity, what is seen as female, and, by extension, women. A necessary step in this process is to encourage men to develop weapons to destroy this part of themselves, in other words, to beat the femininity or the un-man out of men—himself and others. The training is a way to tear the soon-to-be warrior down to the roots, and then "make a new man out of him." "Man," in this context, means being tough, violent, fiercely independent, adult, and heterosexual. Any variance from that rigid and restrictive definition is deemed feminine and therefore need to be eliminated. The evidence suggests that one of the most common places for men to be raped as adults is in the military (see McMullen, *Male Rape*). A purpose of the United States military is to maintain the social order—an order of white male supremacy. Rape, regardless of the gender of the victim/survivor, is a weapon to maintain white male supremacy.

The official training that men receive in preparation for warring behavior prepares us to fight and to kill to protect the "motherland." This training teaches us to accept and use violence and degradation, as well as to stay far removed from other people—particularly emotionally. We are taught to create an image of the "enemy" as not human—as "gook," as "wop," as "jap," or as whatever. This makes it easier to kill, for we aren't killing another human, "just a _____" (you fill in the blank). Therein lies the root of struggling against the use of racist slurs. To use racist slurs refers to times when those races were defined as the "enemy" and were systematically exploited and victimized. The theory and practice of using anti-woman slurs works similarly ("bitch," "dyke," etc.). When using these words, it reminds women of the times (including current times) in which men systematically destroyed and annihilated women.

Military training requires that we lose touch with a piece of our humanity. Those of you who have served know very well what I'm talking about. In order to be willing and prepared to kill another human being, we must disconnect from a part of our own humanity. We have to shut down. It is impossible to be fully and completely human and kill. This training maintains the military ideology of "strength"—and unfortunately, that misinformation is the foundation of our culture as a whole, which raises all men with the knowledge that we may have to go to war. We have to live our lives in this state of semiconnectedness—for if we do have to go to war, we need to know how to totally separate to a point where we can kill. All men internalize these ideas of "strength" and masculinity.

The cost of this training is too high for men. Losing touch with our full humanness means living a part of our lives dead and cold. Life is passionate and irrational. It is fun and joyous and painful and aggravating. It is frustratingly slow, and invigoratingly fast. In order to be fully alive, we have to be able to feel all of this, and tragically, as men, we don't.

In my own life, there are parts of my being that are difficult to get to, to be in touch with, and to express openly. I see it in the lives of the men in my life—my father, my brother, my male colleagues, and my friends. I see it clearly in the men's movement—men trying desperately to reconnect with that part of themselves by going out into the woods and beating on drums. Men who don't like to hug, and aren't comfortable holding hands while walking down the street (unless in a sexual relationship), who don't talk with each other face to face—these men prefer having intense discussions while shooting pool, working on the car, watching the football game. I see men, including myself, who have a very difficult time with the practice of process—always wanting to "get to the point!" That isn't fully living, that isn't being fully alive. This is militaristic thinking at its most internalized.

Given the amount of men's violence against women, clearly the mindset used to perpetrate men's wars is also prevalent during so-called peacetime. This training goes beyond the official training grounds. All men get these same messages, in different and perhaps in more subtle ways. We get the same messages from the play ground ("What are you, some kind of girl?") to movies for adults only ("Hickory dickory dock, your wife was sucking my cock. The clock struck two, I dropped my goo, I kicked the bitch down the fucking block."—Andrew Dice Clay in his 1991 movie *Dice Rules*). We are taught these messages in music, in commercials, and by watching our parents interact. All men are taught to hate femininity and to project images of masculinity out into the world. In order to truly "be a man," men must be willing to destroy what is feminine—in ourselves and in the world.

Women are killed and otherwise victimized more frequently by their allies than by their "enemies." Women are more often raped by the men in their lives; beaten more often by their partners; harassed most commonly by their co-workers, fellow students or bosses; and killed almost always by their husbands or boyfriends. A woman's visit to the hospital is more often the result of being beaten by the man who supposedly loves her than any other single reason—including car accidents, heart attacks, and rape *combined*. Men don't discard the military training we receive on the battlegrounds or the playgrounds; instead we carry it with us back to the streets, and our offices, our classrooms, and most commonly, into our bedrooms. Given this evidence, our collective efforts to destroy the un-man in each of us is slowly and deliberately destroying the very universe we live in—all in the name "being a man."

The two levels of training from the militaristic mindset converge. Teaching men to hate women, on the one hand, and to dissociate from ourselves, each other, and the planet, on the other, creates a climate in which woman killing is natural. When we are this disconnected from our own selves, and our complete humanness, we have no difficulty attacking "others," and we have great difficulty understanding the level of pain of rape survivors. Further, when women are killed or otherwise victimized, because we have been so dissociated and because we have been taught that "women are supposed to be raped," we consistently don't respond in an appropriate or effective manner.

## MEN'S JEALOUSY

Women *appear* to have a monopoly on life, since the process of pregnancy and giving birth is unique to women. Although many men spend a great deal of energy and effort being actively involved in the birth process, we are still separated. We are separated physically by the stomach lining, emotionally by the bonding that occurs between mother and fetus, and spiritually by our own distance from children. Regardless of how close we, as individuals, want and work to become involved in the birth process, we are still separated. As painful, frustrating, and disappointing as that truth is, we all know it to be true. Many of us know the joy of feeling the life kick for the first time, yet wonder what it must be like to feel that within our own bodies. We all recognize how we don't understand a friend or loved one's mood swings, back pain, weak bladder, or the constant fatigue as this new life grows inside her. It is the woman's body that changes, her lifestyle that must adjust. It is the bodies of women from which a new life, a new human being, is brought forth.

Men can only be involved from the outside looking in. And with that comes a pain and a sorrow that we all share. However, men have been taught that, to be a "real man," we are supposed to be powerful, and being powerful means being in control. Men aren't, and can't be, in control of the birth process (regardless of how hard we may try to be). Many men can and do become very involved in the birth and rearing of children. However, until the woman gives birth, the level of involvement and control that men have is severely limited.

Men's response to the apparent dilemma of having no control over something they want control over appears to have been threefold: taking control over death and destruction, thereby appearing to "balance the power"; dominating and controlling women and children, thereby creating the illusion of control over life; and creating a series of god-like images in our image, thereby creating a mystique that those like us possess ultimate control of all life—in other words, "omnipotence."

## Male Control of Death

In response to the sense that women are in control of life via childbirth, men have created a position for ourselves of being the ultimate controllers of death and destruction. We spend billions and billions of dollars and endless amounts of mental and emotional energy on weapons in order to prove just how good we are at killing and destroying. When not preparing for war, going to war, or recovering from war, we seem inept and out of place. We have created weapons with unbelievable power to destroy—up to and including the entire planet and everything on it several hundred times over. We are indeed "good" at it.

Being able to destroy all life certainly *feels* like control. To be able to destroy whatever is in our way (including human beings), to be able to kill with such relative ease, to be in charge, with the touch of a button, of this awesome "power" certainly creates an illusion of being in control. As long as being able to destroy all life as we know it is defined as "power," and being able to control that power is part of "being a man," men will continue to maintain our stranglehold on violence.

## Women as Men's Property

"Being a man" means being able to express our power and authority *over* other people. "A man's home is his castle," and much of the American legal tradition and our social practices is based on the assumption that what happens within a man's home is for him to decide. He has control over those who also reside in his "kingdom"—"his" wife and children. A prime example is the issue of marital rape. At the time of this writing, most states have some level of marital exemption for rape (only two have complete exemptions). This means that the state's rape laws don't apply if the couple is married. Most states recognize some form of rape between married couples, but most also have some exemptions. For example, rape is not considered to be rape in legal terms, in some states, unless the couple has filed for divorce or is living apart. Or sometimes, legal rape only occurs when the woman suffers extreme levels of violence. In effect, the marriage license is seen as a license to rape.

By taking control of women and children, men position ourselves as controlling life itself. Women appear to control life, the thinking goes. Therefore if men control women—particularly women's reproductive capabilities—then men are able to control the bodies through which life comes. The clearest examples of this paradigm are the current attempts by men to reduce women's reproductive options. By trying to limit the control women have over their own bodies and lifestyles, men can effectively create the sense of gaining control over life itself.

Additionally, men are in a position within patriarchy to define "reality." So, as long as we can define the terms, we can create a logic to justify our behavior. Marielouise Janssen-Jureit wrote in *Sexism: The Male Monopoly on History and Thought* that patriarchy created a system by which we can justify continued male control. For example, according to a widely believed and overused myth, a hero will come for every woman—some dashing and brave young man who will sweep by on his valiant steed and carry the damsel away to safety and undying love. Wrapped throughout this myth and the countless variations thereof is male control: a man steering the valiant steed, a man defining what safety is for the damsel in distress, and a man choosing where they will find safety and a place to experience their undying love. And don't forget, it was men who created the myth in the first place—yet another example of male control.

By defining women and children as the property of men, men have created a system in which violence makes total sense. In a capitalist system, a "man" must be willing to fight, even kill for his property. This ideology certainly extends to women and children as men's property. How many men are willing to fight another man who "looks at his woman"? Or is it to protect his own image? We frequently see men's violence also directed at women who attempt to leave a relationship—women are frequently killed by their husbands or boyfriends when trying to leave a relationship. And I'm sure we've all heard men say, "If I can't have you, no one can." Or, less violent but certainly no less controlling: "You must be crazy to leave me. Don't you know how good I am?"

## Men Creating Male Deities

Patriarchy is marked by hierarchy. When men create a deity (or series of deities) in our image, we are able to use that one-upmanship to justify our controlling of women's lives. By creating deities as omnipotent, omniscient, all knowing, all powerful—and as male—men then claim a kinship with those deities. Many traditional religions which have male deities maintain and reinforce men in the upper echelon of their religion's hierarchy. By claiming this unique relationship, men are able to justify the maintenance of the "all boys club" and continue our domination over women. Perhaps the clearest example of this is the Catholic Church and its absolute unwillingness to ordain women as priests—by claiming that men are in God's image and are better able to meet the needs of the parishioners. This is of course of a piece with its position against allowing women to control their own reproductive options. Through this method, men are able to explain women's apparent monopoly over life and still maintain a sense of being a man and in control. Under this rationale, it is even a man (God the Father) who put women on this planet in the first place and who gave them their unique skill of childbearing.

All of these responses to men's lack of control over life are used to justify, explain, and express men's violence. Not only do they fall short in their own right, but they all give men total license, and total justification, for oppression, domination, control, and violence. By claiming to be in total control (male bonding with God), and by controlling women's bodies and lives while developing our skills at violence and killing, we have created a dynamic in which rape is natural and necessary.

## "POWER" AND POWER

Power as traditionally defined by patriarchy is seen as limited, external, and insatiable. Power is something that one has *over* another (i.e., "control") and something that, although never clearly defined, must be used. Power has become synonymous with control. To be a "real man," one must have some demonstrable control over somebody else—and thus be "powerful." Violence, and the threat thereof, is a main method of demonstrating one's control and, thus, one's power.

True power, as opposed to what we've been taught, is a multidimensional entity. Real power is innate, internal, and unlimited. We all are powerful beings—naturally. We all have the ability to choose how we are going to live our lives based on what is most true for us. As human beings, we have the singular ability in the animal kingdom to choose how to direct our life. *That* is power! The power of choice means that not only can we directly impact our own lives and the lives of those around us (based on how we choose to live our lives), but we can, and do, have an impact on the entire universe.

Power comes from a place deep inside yourself. It isn't attached to a position or a talent or a mindset. Rather, power is about being. Being powerful means knowing deep within yourself who you are, and living your life as an expression and celebration of who you are. This means consciously choosing how you want to express your true inner self and doing so. Notice that there's *nothing* about control anywhere in this definition.

However, because we exist in a patriarchy, most of us have internalized the understanding of power as control, and it becomes very difficult to completely divorce ourselves from that understanding. To add to this difficulty, control has external benefits attached to it. Being wealthy, for example, is defined as "powerful" in this culture. Those who have money are given a number of benefits due to the amount of money they have. And it grows exponentially. People with a little money have a little power; people with a lot of money have a lot more power. The "power" that these people have may not have anything to do with who they are as individuals, and may be solely attached to the wealth that they happen to be connected to.

Resorting to the use of violence demonstrates being controlling, or having "power over" in a particular situation, but it doesn't express a sense of true power. Violence is generally a response to feeling very out of control. It's clear in examples all over the place. When former President Bush ordered the troops to begin bombing Iraq, it was because he felt that Saddam Hussein was "out of control" (read, out of George Bush's control). But dropping bombs didn't work. Saddam Hussein is still there and is still "out of control." Men who batter frequently report the same pattern. Being a man requires being able to control another person, and if we are feeling out of control, we are taught to reclaim control by getting violent. The patterns runs something like this:

I am a man and therefore I'm supposed to be in control. I'm feeling out of control, so I'll grab hold of this person's hand to demonstrate that I am in control. But it's not working, she isn't under my control yet (she can still move her hand, as well as move the rest of her body; and she can also think, feel, talk, etc.). I feel more desperate to get her under control, but I am feeling more out of control due to having to resort to such an inane attempt at being powerful.

These two contradictory patterns then kick in together and exacerbate the feelings of being out of control:

So I grab hold tighter, or with my other hand, or whatever. But it still doesn't work. But to be a "man" I'm supposed to be "in control," and this is the only way I know to be in control, but I'm losing control of myself and this situation (because I have to grab tighter and harder and become more expressive or violent). But this is the only way I know how to take control so I need to get bigger and more controlling but it doesn't work.

It isn't much longer before someone is hitting, raping, or dropping a bomb somewhere—still feeling like he has no control. This same scenario is described, in different ways, countless times by men who batter, parents who abuse children, and men who express oppressiveness over others by violent means. As one batterer put it: "She wasn't listening to me so I had to regain control of her. She just kept yelling and wouldn't listen to me."

Furthermore, we are driven to rather far-reaching extremes in attempts to protect the control we feel we do have, however limited that may be. Capitalism affects much of our mentality, and we are taught to "protect" those things that we cherish, those entities of value we own. One way to protect ourselves and our property is to be willing to be violent. This, too, is part of "being a man."

## MEN'S ROLE AS VIOLATOR, WOMEN'S ROLE AS VICTIM

Men are taught to be a certain way and to fill certain roles, women certain others. For the most part, these roles are and have traditionally been diametrically opposed to each other. Men tend to be defined and evaluated by what we do rather than who we are. Our role is that of protector and provider, as well as that of conqueror. Men are traditionally responsible for making sure that "our" women and children are provided for and safe. Since little in nature threatens women and children anymore, men have responded by creating a larger threat than any other, as a way of maintaining our role in society. We have created ourselves as the threat that women and children need to be protected from.

The theories espoused by the male fundamentalists, most notably by Robert Bly, are problematic and dangerous on a number of levels. Firstly, their dismissal of feminism and attempts to paint women and mothers as the reason for men's pain is misguided and inappropriate. Further, his analysis begins from a place of women and men being "separate but equal" and argues that men have become "too much in touch with our women side" and need to get back to our "true" inner masculinity. Additionally, his image of "true masculinity" is very Euro-biased and therefore racist, and extremely heterosexist. Finally, his work does not benefit men. He encourages men to reclaim masculinity without offering a critique of the ways that masculinity has hurt men. Going into the woods and beating on a drum may feel good for a weekend. But men have to live in *this* world in *this* time. We don't need to get back to an unhealthy image of manhood, no matter how good it feels. We need to recreate masculinity—and we are strong and powerful enough to do so—not celebrate that which is killing us and that which we use to kill off "others" and the planet itself*

Women are also defined externally by men who have set up the system of evaluation and conditioning. The ways that women are defined as "good" or "bad" are, for the most part, based on male definitions (man is the norm, woman is an aberration thereof). Women are primarily defined based on their physical appearance or their connection to a man (daddy's girl, husband's wife, son's mother, and so on). Women's traditional role is that of care-taker, a part of whose responsibility is to put one's own needs on hold while working to take care of the others. This role is compounded for women of color and working-class women who not only are supposed to take care of the men in their lives, but also white men and wealthier men.

These divergent roles set up a dynamic which places women at increased risk for victimization in a number of ways: men are the primary actors, women respond to them; men "protect," which puts women at risk because they "need" a man to protect them; and men, by virtue of being the "protector," are taught to fight and hit, while women are not. Bottom line: our society has set men up to be the victimizers or at least to be perceived as the victimizer, while setting women up to be victimized. This

---

*For a further critique, see *Women Respond to the Men's Movement: A Feminist Collection*, ed. by Kay Leigh Hagan (New York: HarperCollins, 1992) and *Backlash: The Undeclared War Against Women*, by Susan Faludi (New York: Crown Books).

isn't to say that some men aren't victimized, and that some women aren't violent. But according to the norms of our culture as well as the extent of the violence perpetrated by men, the roles have been set along these gender lines. In order to have an impact on ending men's violence, we *must* redefine these roles.

# FOUR

# MEN WORKING TO STOP RAPE

*What Gets in the Way?*

BECAUSE YOU ARE still reading, I take that to mean that you are ready to commit to confronting men's violence. Sadly, that puts you in the minority. Most men, even the men who are considered allies to women and feminists, do painfully little to address and confront the issues of men's violence. Because you are still reading, I think it's safe to assume that you've been doing some serious thinking. And it hasn't been easy. Any time spent examining a truth as ugly as rape will make one experience some of the ugliness. The added topics of adultism, racism, and homophobia only act to further intensify what is already difficult, complicated, and emotionally painful. I've asked you to critically reexamine some of the basic tenets of what you've probably taken very much for granted for most of your life: "being a man," the meaning of masculinity, sex, power, control, and sexual orientation. That process is never easy.

I hope I've been somewhat successful in defining the problems, but the struggle for a rape-free culture requires more than this. Struggling for a rape-free culture requires that we begin defining solutions, and begin working to implement these solutions. From here on is where that happens. Here is where we get serious, and I hope have a little more fun. The rest of the book will identify some of the barriers to men taking action, discuss empowerment, examine some proposed solutions, and focus on ways that men can take direct and personal action for stopping rape.

## WHAT ARE OUR FEELINGS AS
## WE BEGIN TO DO ANTI-RAPE WORK?

One of the primary purposes of this book is to encourage you to begin recognizing that the personal tragedy of rape happens within a sociocultural, political, and personal context. I have tried, through the last three chapters, to define the context within which men rape. In this context violence is eroticized, and control is sexualized; in it much of how we are defined as "men" has to do with maintaining our position of domination and "one-upmanship" over what I have described as un-men.

In this next chapter, I look specifically at what happens when one, especially one who is male, begins to recognize rape culture. The political is personal just as much as the "personal is political" (as the feminist slogan goes), and recognizing rape culture does have a personal impact.

Recognizing rape culture is frequently a slow process. As we begin identifying its impacts on women, we begin to squirm uncomfortably. Yet we also recognize the extent to which women are affected, and the ways that we have in the past and continue to act in ways that support rape culture.

Most of us don't know what it's like to live our lives constantly aware of the threats that are waiting for us. Few of us know what it is like to not take a walk to the neighborhood store at night for fear of being attacked. This lack of knowledge isn't universally true. Gay men have some level of fear; men of color certainly know neighborhoods where it isn't safe; and for most male children, there is a level of knowledge about some ill-defined but seemingly ever-present threat of adult male strangers. However, women are uniformly affected more than the men of the same class, age, or racial background. There *is* a gender disparity.

When men begin to see this gender disparity, we are often hesitant and avoid our own insights. Most of us respond with a level of denial. "How could it be?" we say to ourselves. Or, "How can so many women be victimized so often and I be so oblivious to it all?" we holler. We try to deny what is so obviously true, knowing all the time, at some level, that we truthfully can't deny it. In a part of ourselves that we rarely acknowledge, we *know* that this rape culture exists. We have difficulty coming to terms with that—for if it is true that this is a rape culture, then most of what we believe about this culture is thrown into question. And *that* is scary, not to mention overwhelming.

As we continue our struggle, we begin to recognize that our silence has spoken volumes and has acted as support for the continual violence. Those first feelings of responsibility are generally filled with intense guilt, shame, and a morass of often overwhelming emotions. We often don't know how to handle the emotions and the intensity of what we're facing and aren't sure where to go with them.

At least for a time, most of us try to hide from these feelings and this awareness. We try to minimize the impact this growing consciousness has on us. We attempt to blow it off as not as important as it really is. We want, desperately, to keep our position and stay comfortable—but we are living a constant contradiction. It's hard to have as good a time watching stupid movies, and just being silly about them when you've begun to recognize the sexism, racism, homophobia, and violence so prevalent in these stupid movies, and the rest of what we have come to call "entertainment," and the ways that we have traditionally been "silly." It becomes difficult to enjoy oneself when remembering stories about the violence women experience and survive, and seeing examples everywhere you go.

As this happens, unfortunately, our coping mechanisms take some time to respond. After all, this is a new experience, so we are often left to deal with this all but constant bombardment of new information, experiences, interpretations and feelings with skills that aren't quite up to speed. The result is that we are frequently left flailing—not sure how to be, how to act, and what we're feeling (much less how to express it). It isn't fun! But we can and do live through it!

Men beginning to see rape culture also often experience a general feeling of despondency. It is very difficult and downright painful to see rape this intensely. When we first begin to look at these issues, we rarely have the skills necessary to effectively deal with the emotions that are stirred up. Until we develop those skills, and establish the framework to put these feelings into a context, as well as create patterns for keeping ourselves healthful in the process, we are left to our own devices. Most men don't have access to our feelings, don't have the words to label the feelings we have, or know how to reach out for help in ways that will be meaningful when we are struggling. And it is within this troubled context that we begin to see rape culture. Clearly, this leaves us in a place of difficulty.

To further compound these feelings, most men who begin recognizing rape culture experience isolation. Even the tenuous hold we have on our relationship with other men becomes threatened as we begin looking with different eyes. We question behaviors that we used to join in. We are no longer able to hang out with our men friends in the same ways that we used to. There aren't a whole lot of men doing this kind of work, or who are developing this kind of understanding, and we are left feeling like we're all alone.

At the same time, we find ourselves surrounded more and more by women who very much like what we are saying and doing. But they still aren't men. Their experiences and life situations are very different from those of men. They may be very supportive, encouraging, and caring, but there is no way for them to understand what it is we are going through. Doing this work *is* isolating—at least initially!

Finally, seeing rape culture often feels more overwhelming than anything we've ever experienced before. It's everywhere. And as we get better at seeing it, we get better at seeing it being everywhere—the subtle expressions, the intonations, the hints of sexism and violence that for so long we've been willing and able to brush off without a second thought. Now, they stick. Now, we have those second thoughts, and we aren't sure where to go with them. "So now I've gotten good at seeing sexism—it's everywhere and I can now see how prevalent it is. So what?"

The "so what" is that now we can begin *doing something* about it. You can't do anything if you don't see what's staring you in the face. When you begin seeing what's wrong, we can begin working towards solutions. Unfortunately, it often takes a while between seeing the problem and beginning to see solutions.

Living an anti-rape lifestyle; confronting racism, heterosexism, adult-ism; and working for nonviolence has resulted in the most meaningful, powerful, and important relationships that I've had. My friendships now are with men and women of all ages, colors, backgrounds, sexual orientations, classes, and physical and mental abilities. As a direct result of doing the work that I do, I have come to realize just how out of touch we as men tend to be. It is by doing radical, pro-feminist social change work that I have come to a place of being fully human, more fully human than any amount of counseling, therapy, or self-help programs that I could have possibly participated in. Most of the men who are living anti-oppression lifestyles report similar experiences. It *is* a struggle. But rest assured you will get through. Many of us have as well.

## WHAT KEEPS US FROM ACTING?

Men have not historically responded effectively to men's violence. As women have worked to develop rape crisis centers, to define and expand the understanding of rape, and to develop training programs supporting rape survivors and preventing rape, men have either gotten in the way, or been silent. As women have done the amazing work that they've done, most men have been silent and inactive. It has only been when men's sexual violence has impacted directly on the lives of men, either in the form of attacks on their friends, or accusations made against their friends, that men have taken any action at all. By and large, the most active and eloquent men have been the men who have acted as *barriers* to eliminating rape, for example, by questioning the rape statistics, criticizing the rape prevention programs organized by feminists, and denying funding for rape crisis centers. These issues were raised very publicly again in the early 1990s with the rape trials of William Kennedy Smith and Mike Tyson, and the sexual harassment allegations against Supreme Court nominee Clarence Thomas, and Senators Bob Packwood (Oregon) and Daniel Inouye (Hawaii). During this time, the nation's newspapers were flooded with op-ed pieces and letters to the editors that dramatized men's resistance: women wrote that they believed the accusations and shared their own experiences; men ignored the accusations or questioned the victim—"Why did she take her panty hose off?" "Why did she follow him to the Equal Employment Opportunities Commission?" "Why did she wait so long to come forward?" Irrelevant in the first place, these questions place the responsibility for the victimization on the survivor, rather than focusing on the inappropriateness of the behavior of the accused.

The fact that men haven't responded in any kind of proactive and effective manner could lead one to ask, "Why?" Why are men not responding? Why are men finding it so difficult to determine that these issues are worth responding to? Why is it, despite the rhetoric of men who claim to be opposed to rape, that rape continues to increase, that rape crisis programs continue to struggle for enough funding to meet the demand, and that when specific cases arise, men continue to doubt and blame the victim/survivor (female or male)? I don't have the answers to these questions, only more questions. But perhaps by examining these questions and the others, we, as men, can come up with some solutions.

Before I begin that process, however, one final point. As men, we are inherently creative; we have unlimited intelligence. As we've demonstrated before, there is very little that we can't do if we put our minds, our energy, and our commitment to it. I believe that the same is true with men's violence. If and when we put our minds, our energy, and our commitment to working with feminists to eliminate rape, we *will* stop rape.

There are a number of reasons why men haven't responded to men's sexual violence: these issues seem boring, or we don't know how to respond, or we haven't felt like a place for us existed in the movement. Also, feelings of shame and guilt arise. And we don't know other men who have been working on these issues, and therefore we feel fearful and isolated, afraid of doing "the wrong thing." We also don't want to really challenge other men (which truly is very scary), can't bear to seriously challenge ourselves and give up our privilege. And we feel like we have to "give up" something in order to do this work and don't know what will replace whatever it is that we are giving up.

## NOT KNOWING HOW/ISOLATION

Perhaps the greatest of these barriers is not knowing what to do to stop rape or how to live an anti-rape lifestyle. There haven't been a whole lot of models of men doing effective and proactive work against sexual violence. Since the early days of the movement, a handful of men have been acting in support of women. Overwhelmingly, however, these men have been acting on the sidelines, and have been only marginally visible. As a result, we can discern little tradition of men's involvement in the movement, and we are left without models as to what form that involvement could take. The vast majority of the people we see doing work on issues of sexual violence are women. The men who we have seen involved tend to come from a legal perspective (lawyers, police, judges, politicians), and as such tend to come to these issues from a very different perspective and offer legal solutions (such as supporting more prisons, stiffer penalties), rather than the more broadly based and effective solutions that are needed (educational programs, training for men).

The only other men we've seen doing anything are those men who actively deny what feminist leaders are saying about rape, and to minimize the impact of anti-rape work. As a result, men who have wanted to get involved haven't known what to do—haven't seen what it would look like to be a man against rape. Having models from which to build is essential. We all need examples of others who do what it is that we want to do. The same is true for doing anti-rape work. When all we see are men doing nothing, or doing things that aren't what we're interested in doing (such as lobbying or building prisons), it increases the difficulty of doing anti-rape work.

Most of the men who work to confront and eliminate men's violence discuss the feelings of isolation they feel or have felt. Most of us have found that our closest friends are women—and yet, there is a difference. As sympathetic, caring, and understanding as I may be, I can not *share* the experience of being a woman and growing up female in this culture. I grew up male. That is a world of differences! To pretend as if those differences don't exist is to lie. At the same time, I don't quite fit with the "boys" anymore. By the same token, women don't share my experience of growing up male and being a man working against male privilege. As supportive and caring as they are, they can't share my experiences. That requires other men who are sharing my experiences—men who are living an anti-sexist, nonviolent lifestyle.

Feelings of isolation make it extremely difficult to move, even when you know that you want to. It's a challenge to find your way when you don't have people who share your experience. That is part of the power of the feminist consciousness-raising (CR) process. CR groups offer women an opportunity to come together as women with a shared experience and talk with each other about being women. It broke the isolation and created an environment in which movement and growth could and did occur. By and large, men have not created similar opportunities for ourselves and each other. This isn't to say that some men haven't grown and developed. Movement is simply much more difficult to do in isolation. Men have let that isolation and the threat of becoming isolated become a barrier to doing anti-rape work.

For example, when I first became active, in Texas, only a handful of men were doing any kind of anti-violence work, mostly working with men who batter. Now, Texas is a very big state, and we were all quite isolated. We would see each other at conferences and at other events from time to time, but generally we were each on our own. I pretty much had to create my own process as I went along. It was scary, it was difficult, and I made a lot of mistakes. At the same time, I was living in an all-male dorm, and getting lots of proddings to give up my work and revert to the old ways of "being a man." The only support that I received to keep doing what I needed to be doing was from the feminists with whom I was working—and to some extent, from a few other women on campus. When I finally found other men who were doing this work, and whom I could share with and learn from, it became indescribably easier. I could check out what I was thinking with other men who had also had those thoughts and with whom I shared the experience of growing up male in this culture. It made the process easier, and made me more able and willing to take new and bolder steps.

## FEMINISTS' "HESITANCY"

As if isolation alone weren't enough, this isolation is further complicated by what many men feel is an unwillingness of the feminist movements to include men. It should be immediately noted that this so-called hesitancy is minimal when compared to the lack of interest men have traditionally shown to these issues, and the lack of effort men have displayed in becoming proactively involved in confronting rape or supporting these same feminists' efforts against rape. Furthermore, the "hesitancy" of feminists has been well founded, based on concerns that men would continue to act out traditional patriarchal conditioning such as taking over—which we've done. "Gentler, kinder" taking over is still taking over.

Most of us, as men, don't know how to follow the leadership and the direction of women—or of other men, for that matter. We have all learned to respond to a situation by "fixing it"—by figuring out what needs to be done, taking over, and doing what needs to be done. We've learned that to "be a man" we're supposed to take over and resolve the situation. In and of themselves, these tactics aren't necessarily wrong, but they become problematic when in a context of working to confront issues of men taking control via a process of men taking control. Men haven't learned a lot of skills of process (i.e., how to proceed towards getting things done). Something very powerful can be said about learning skills of what has been traditionally described as "following."

Men also tend to look to feminists to determine what our role in the movement is. Yet it isn't up to women to determine what should be the role of men in working to end men's violence. We must set up processes where we interact in respectful and responsive ways with the feminist leadership and where we establish the trust necessary for us to work effectively together. But it is up to us as men to develop that trust as well as to determine our role(s) in this movement: As several feminist activists have told me, "It's up to you, you men to create ways for men to be involved. It isn't up to us to figure out how you fit in."

Men who get involved tend to want to be supported and applauded by women and feminists for the work that we do. We seem to feel that we are trying, therefore we should receive some accolade. As one feminist leader told me when I was first starting, "Don't expect applause for taking out the trash. Rape is your trash. I'm not going to pat you on the back for doing what you should have been doing all along." I want to be explicitly clear: Men shouldn't be doing anti-rape work to get patted on the back by women. We need to do this work, as I've described, because this is our work and because it benefits men for us to do this work.

## MEN'S ANGER AND OTHER FEELINGS

A further barrier to men's involvement is not knowing how to deal with men's anger. We have all seen the ways that men's anger gets directed at women and we, very legitimately, don't want to be the front for men's anger. We fear that if and when we confront other men on their behavior and attitudes, they will get angry with us. Men *do* get angry when confronted. But if we think of our own process, we remember that most of us have been confronted ourselves. And there were probably quite a few times when we responded by getting angry. Reexamining the ways we responded to being confronted can give us some insight into how other men may respond when confronted. Men will and do get angry.

Doing anti-rape work, however, does not mean agreeing to take responsibility for men's anger. For example, several years ago I gave a speech at Duke University in North Carolina. As I was nearing the end of my presentation, I was interrupted by a very angry man—so angry he was shaking—who yelled about my "man-hating" and how I had obviously been "brainwashed by those radical, ball-busting feminists." He made a number of threatening gestures towards me (thankfully he was further back in the audience) and continued for several moments. Clearly not interested in a dialogue, he was rather responding to a number of things I had said: that men's violence was *men's*, that all men had to take responsibility for the violence and for stopping the violence, and men can work in some clear and concrete ways to stop the violence. One of the things he said during his diatribe was how he "wasn't responsible for all the bad things all men do!" I was shaken by that confrontation. It scared me, and it angered me. Even now, with as many presentations and trainings as I've done, I still have anxieties about what to do with men's responses—I'm still scared every time I do a presentation.

Men can handle being angry. Men have the skills and the abilities to deal with being angry and to express their anger without being abusive. As presenters, activists, or the person in the bar who's confronting sexism, we don't have to take responsibility for men's anger. Their anger is all theirs. It may be helpful to remember that their anger is at the message, not the messenger. They'll attempt to point their anger at us because we are present and available. But we can choose whether or not we're willing to take on their anger. Generally, it makes little sense for us to take responsibility for their anger. We have enough to be responsive to and for with the issues and with our own feelings about the issues without adding men's anger on as well.

A final note about men's abusiveness: Men can and at times do become verbally abusive in their anger, up to and including threatening physical violence. It is not common, but it does happen. In those situations it is important to do what you need to do to be safe. In those programs that you are organizing, you also have some responsibility for the other participants. Label what is going on ("You're being threatening"), let him know it is unacceptable and what you're feeling ("I'm feeling scared of you and this is not the way to interact with me"), and offer a solution ("Let's take five" or "I'm going to ask you to either calm yourself down, or leave").

A feeling related to the fear of men's anger is the fear of being kicked out of the boys' club. For so many men, there is a sense of only tenuously being "one of the guys." Most of us have grown up feeling a part of the group, but always knowing that "being a part" could end at any moment with little or no warning. Confronting men on sexism and exposing men's misogyny feels like being a traitor (as well it should—it is), and we often fear that we'll be kicked out for traitorously not acting like "one of the guys."

Other barriers come from the feelings the situation creates. One of these has to do with the intensity of our own feelings. It is not at all uncommon for men to be hesitant about doing anti-rape work because we don't know how to deal with the strength of our own feelings. This dynamic strikes particularly true for men who know someone who they know has been raped. We tend to fear that we will "lose it" when confronted by some of the extreme blaming-the-victim dynamics that can arise. We are also concerned that we won't be able to maintain the level of "professionalism" that we "should" have when doing a presentation or a training. Or that we'll get "too emotional" when confronting our male friends on their behaviors or attitudes. We, as men, need to get away from the idea that "getting too emotional" is wrong. It's okay, even good, to get emotional—and to share the emotions we're experiencing. Rape is an extremely intense and emotional topic. Any feeling person is going to feel something when discussing these issues. Let people know that you are feeling emotional. Own it, claim it, revel in it, display it proudly! Anger is not necessarily a bad emotion. Like all our other emotions, it is necessary. Anger is a great motivator and a powerful energizer. The issue isn't whether or not we're going to get angry; the issue is how we express our anger. It's perfectly acceptable to let people know you are angry at what they've said or done.

## WOMEN'S ANGER

Another barrier to men confronting rape is the anger that we may get from women. As difficult and complicated as it is to respond to men's anger, it is nothing when compared to trying to figure out how to respond to women's anger. Women's anger seems primarily to come from one of two places: Either we do something to make women angry, or we are a man who is available for women's anger.

When we do something, or don't do something, that women respond to with anger, responding is much easier (not easy, but easier). We need to look at what we've done or said and see how to take responsibility for whatever happened. Usually an apology is a good place to begin, but it can't end there. We need to listen to what we've done that caused the anger, and continue to dialogue to find resolution. At times that is easier said than done. There will always be times when we disagree with someone and anger is part of the disagreement. But we can always act in ways that are responsive.

When we are a "trigger" for women's anger, it is much more complicated. Intellectually, we may know that the anger isn't directed at us personally. But that can be very difficult to detect while we're in the moment of being confronted. It's important to be prepared for this, because it will happen. Very often, women have never had the experience of having men available to hear their anger—and reasons proliferate for women to be holding a lot of anger. By doing anti-rape work, we're talking about the very issues that may be at the core of this rage. It's important to find the balance between listening and being supportive without being or sounding like a therapist. Even if you have therapist training, this isn't a "session" and that dynamic is not appropriate. We can't take care of ourselves if we become dumping grounds.

A useful place to begin is to identify your own reactions to anger and being confronted. It may not be appropriate to share with her what you're feeling, but you need to notice it. Are your feelings coming from a place that is guarded and defensive (which is certainly understandable), or are your feelings coming from a place of being supportive (these aren't necessarily mutually exclusive)? If they are coming from a place of defensiveness, notice that, be aware of why you're feeling defensive, and respond with that awareness. If your feelings are coming more from a place of being supportive, check in with her to see what she wants from you.

Regardless, it is often helpful to find out from her what she wants from you in relation to her anger. Try to listen beneath what she's saying, and how she's acting, to hear where her anger is coming from. Responding to that can frequently de-escalate the situation.

## BEING ARTICULATE

Another barrier to men taking action is that we aren't particularly articulate about rape, aren't sure how to "get our foot in the door," and don't know how to raise the points. Anytime we feel inarticulate and unable to clearly express ourselves, we are less likely to raise the point. Often most of us carry a sense that someone somewhere knows the issues better, has thought them through more, and has developed his analysis and argument more concretely. We use that belief to stay quiet. Well, rest your fears. There are, in fact, people who are far more articulate than you or I—men who have developed their analysis to a fuller extent and who sound better when they speak. However, just because that is true doesn't mean that there isn't value and necessity in each one of us speaking out. Rather than compare yourself to others, focus on *your* skills and abilities to be articulate about these issues. Generally, those men "who are more articulate" aren't around when the opportunities arise to confront them. Since we are likely the only ones around who are going to speak up, then we've just become the most articulate persons around.

The only way to learn to be articulate is to do it. The more often we practice confronting rape-supporting behaviors and labeling racesexism (the dynamics of racism and sexism are so parallel and so interconnected, that I sometimes name it as one dynamic), the better able we become at confronting rape and labeling racesexism. Even when we don't know if what we're seeing is rape-supporting, we can express that. We can say, "I'm not sure but there's something here that makes me uncomfortable." "I don't like what I'm hearing. I don't know why, or what it is that I don't like, but I don't like it." It really is okay to be "only" semi-articulate. Having "all the answers" is part of traditional male training, we've used the dynamic of needing to have *all* the answers in situations when we don't has worked effectively to keep us silent. We believe that because we don't have all the answers we shouldn't say anything at all. It is not our responsibility to necessarily force agreement. It is our responsibility to confront and label the attitudes that support or tolerate abusive behaviors.

A related but somewhat different issue is when we fear that we are less articulate than those we are challenging. Part of what gets difficult when confronting these kinds of issues is the belief that others are better able to argue their point than we are at arguing ours. As such, if we get into a debate or an argument, he'll "win." But this isn't a contest and the point is not to "win." The point is to raise the issues. Creating a situation in which others must explain their point is in itself valuable. Getting people to agree is certainly nice, but isn't very realistic. Creating an opportunity for men to *think* critically about rape, rape-supporting behaviors, and the related issues is the focus. Even if it's in a "bumbling" way, raising the questions forces people to stop for a moment and think. *That* is valuable.

Regardless of how you raise these points or argue your perspective, the bottom line is to raise these issues. Men working to stop rape are inventing an entirely new process—there aren't a whole lot of guidelines. None of us have all the answers about how to raise these issues effectively. Trust yourself! And just do it. Over time, you will become more articulate, and you will become more comfortable with your skills and your abilities—which in turn increases your ability to be articulate and clear.

## MALE GUILT AND MEN'S DEFENSIVENESS

The guilt, shame, and defensiveness that leaps to the surface for most men even with the mere mention of the words "male violence" acts as yet another barrier to men's involvement. Upon hearing or reading those words, most men respond by claiming that they "aren't violent and most of the men they know aren't violent." Men tend to respond to truthfully labeling sexual violence as *men's* violence by saying that we are suggesting that all men are "bad" or "wrong." This misunderstanding exemplifies the underlying layers of guilt and shame that men feel about issues of rape and sexual violence. By calling it what it is, men's violence, we are only beginning to take an honest look. It is only by taking a truth-seeking, albeit painful look at the problems will we begin finding solutions.

Most counterarguments to anti-rape work come from guilt and shame. The defensiveness that rises up is a cover. When we hear those kinds of arguments—even when they are coming from our own mouths—we need to examine what is underneath and identify the true feelings.

The guilt tends to come from a couple of directions. First off, as we become aware of the extent and level of men's violence, we begin to identify a level of collective guilt for being part of the class that has perpetrated such violence. The dynamic is very similar to white guilt in relation to racism. When we recognize the violence, the levels of oppression, and the depth of the impact on the victims, the feelings are often so overwhelming that feelings of guilt rise to the surface.

On another level, as we become more adept at identifying various forms of men's violence, we become increasingly aware of the more subtle expressions, expressions that most of us have perpetrated in one form or another. If we did an honest appraisal, we would have to identify ways that we too have perpetrated some of this violence. It's hard to look at the ways that we have hurt people, the ways that we've exerted male control to get what we wanted, or the ways that our sexual encounters were full of manipulation and "subtle" pressure so as to get sexual access to women, women we claim to care about. None of us are clean. All of us have used these same skills in order to get what we wanted. We all understand the way the rapist's mind works, because we have all used his mind at one time or another. That acknowledgment often sparks feelings of guilt. It is extremely difficult—although necessary—to maintain a positive and healthful self-image while at the same time acknowledging the ways we have hurt people. We find it much easier to succumb to guilt and respond with defensiveness and hopelessness than to look at the truth, become empowered, and work for change.

The cycle of guilt goes something like this: "Men's violence is bad; all men are violent in some way; therefore all men are bad. All men are bad, I'm a man; therefore I'm bad." Or, "All men are bad—except me." Neither avenue is particularly healthful for men, nor particularly helpful for stopping the violence. Remember that there is a difference between a person and his behavior. It isn't a matter of being "good" or "bad"—it is a matter of being aware of our behavior. None of us has gotten to a point where we are able to claim that we have escaped the teachings and trainings of white patriarchy. We can work on cleaning up our oppressive behaviors, but we haven't succeeded yet. Just as the feminist movement and feminist women are in process, so too is the pro-feminist movement, and are individual men.

All men I know who have begun to develop this awareness work though feelings of guilt and shame, anger and sadness. These words I'm offering are truthfully only that, words, and they may not help a whole lot, but I hope it helps you to hear that people do get through this seemingly endless morass of feelings and intensity.

## PERSONAL BEHAVIOR/ GUILTY RESPONSE-ABILITY

Guilt and response-ability are different. I've tried to focus on and reinforce this point throughout this book. Guilt comes from a place of powerlessness and hopelessness. Guilt is not a true feeling. And guilt is, to a large extent, a cop-out. Guilt does little to change anything, and lots to damage self-esteem. Guilt also, very effectively (and some would argue, manipulatively) keeps the center of attention on "I." By keeping you focused away from the problems, and most certainly away from the potential solutions, guilt shifts you toward thinking about "what a terrible person I am." Guilt also makes us lose track of the fact that there is a difference between a person and his behavior.

When discussing the issues of rape, battery, pornography, incest, harassment, femicide, sexism, racism, and heterosexism, we are discussing behaviors. These forms of violence are behaviors—behaviors that we have learned, and behaviors that we can unlearn. Violence is not innate. Violence is learned and is a choice—not always a conscious choice, but a choice nonetheless, and is therefore our response-ability. As such, the choice to be violent is within our power to make conscious and to interrupt. The choice is two-step: to oppose the violence, and to choose the form that your opposition will take. These choices must become conscious. I submit to you, reading this book, that you are making choices. Even if you choose to put this book down and do nothing more, that is a choice to maintain the status quo—and thereby support rape. Whatever choices you make must be conscious, and must be directed at eliminating men's violence. Additionally, to be effective requires that you make those conscious decisions on a daily basis. Along with your daily meditations of loving yourself, ask yourself how you will confront white male supremacy today!

Guilt, rather than a feeling, is actually a self-centered thought process. In *This Bridge Called My Back*, Cherrie Moraga and Gloria Anzaldua see guilt as *"not* a feeling. It is an intellectual mask of a feeling." Audre Lorde described guilt as "only another way of avoiding informed action, of buying time out of the pressing need to make clear choices, out of the approaching storm that can feed the earth as well as bend the trees." Guilt doesn't work for change, is not liberating, and does little more than destroy your self-image. It's not helpful, and isn't worth it.

Guilt also comes from the past—we are guilty for what we did last week. There is no way to undo what has been done. The best we can do is to look at what we have done, interrupt it, and learn from it so we stop supporting rape in the future.

Almost all of us have been misinformed about the difference between taking responsibility and feeling guilty or ashamed. Most of us learned about responsibility by doing something wrong as a young child. Suddenly, an adult two or three times larger than we are is in our face, very upset, with a finger chiding us or a hand slapping our butt telling us, usually in a loud voice, "Take responsibility for what you've done!" That isn't about taking responsibility; that's about feeling bad and cowering. Most of us have brought those experiences up with us to adulthood. So now whenever we hear "responsibility," we respond the same way we did when we were five: by feeling guilty, cowering, and wanting to run away from here as fast as our legs can carry us. But true responsibility is something very different. Response-ability, as this spelling suggests, is actually about recognizing that we have the "ability to respond" to a situation in a proactive way that improves it. Men have an incredible ability (as yet untapped) to end rape. Response-ability, rather than being being about feeling bad, is actually about empowerment!

To work effectively towards solutions, we all must feel personally response-able (i.e., able to respond). We must feel a personal stake in the problem and in the solutions to engage in constructive problem-solving. Feeling response-able is acknowledging our participation in or support of behavior that has hurt people, coupled with the knowledge that we are capable of responding in a proactive manner towards resolving the hurt. Guilt and shame do not acknowledge these abilities.

Taking full response-ability also means accepting responsibility for the ways that we have hurt people. The twelve steps for recovering from addiction use this same thinking—but, unfortunately, refuse to take this valuable insight into the broader arena of world oppression and politics. Recovering addicts are encouraged to take full responsibility for the ways that they have hurt others while in the middle of their addictive process(es). Guilt is actively discouraged, but taking response-ability is not about taking guilt. It isn't that the addict was "bad" in some inherent way. Rather, the person who is addicted did things that hurt people—and is working to take full responsibility for the hurt he or she has caused, and to make amends for that pain. Guilt only interrupts that process.

As with the addict in addiction, men in a violent society are not the problem. There is absolutely nothing wrong with men. The behavior of violence, and the attitudes that support and encourage men's violence, are the problem. We must keep that distinction clear—a person is more than their behaviors. Just like the addict recognizes that she or he is responsible for the pain and hurt she or he has caused or allowed, so too must men acknowledge the pain and hurt we've perpetrated and allowed. Accepting full response-ability is different than guilt. Accepting response-ability is about empowerment. Accepting full response-ability is about being fully human!

To change and grow, we must take the behaviors personally. We need to acknowledge the ways that we support this system, and move to interrupt our support of male supremacy—that is personal. Changing requires that we take serious stock of who we are and what we believe about ourselves, and that is profoundly personal. And lest we forget, we are talking about rape and other forms of men's violence—that is deeply personal, as the feminist movement has continuously reminded us.

Women have responded to men's violence personally. Most women, as has been discussed, go to some rather extraordinary lengths every day in response to men's violence and its threat. So common and frequent are these adjustments that when asked, many women will not consciously know what they do. The challenge for us as men, who claim to be supportive of women, is to make *one* conscious choice a day about how we will adjust our lives as a result of the threat of rape and to confront it. Take the personal responsiblity to create one pattern a day in response to rape.

## BEING "HYPOCRITICAL"

Another barrier against action that arises frequently is the sense of being hypocritical: "How can I confront men on these issues when just last week I was doing similar things?" we think. This concern arises most directly in response to the continuum of sexism I discussed previously. Men will say, "If I'm on the continuum, where do I get off talking with other men about rape?" Well, it's important to acknowledge that we are all somewhere on the continuum. However, it is also true that we are in process—the value is in acknowledging that we are in process, and in what we're learning to see, not in holding ourselves up as some kind of example.

It is not at all uncommon to be challenged by men about our own harassing and sexist behaviors. For example, I have harassed women at times and people have called me on it. We need to acknowledge the hurtful and abusive behaviors that we've done *and* reemphasize that we're not talking about "bad" men but rather hurtful behaviors. Yes, I have harassed women. I've also tried to be accountable and take responsibility for that and have stopped doing it. But having harassed women doesn't necessarily make me a "bad" person in the same way that doing anti-rape work doesn't necessarily make me a "good" person. All of us do some good things, and some not-so-good things. The point is not to be un-sexist/racist/homophobic/ageist/etc. (for that is impossible); the point is that we as men can confront our own behaviors and those of our brothers to make the world a more worthwhile place to live—for *all of us!*

Men have a lot to gain from ending rape culture. It is of more benefit to us individually and socially to end rape than it is to continue to support rape culture. Within rape culture men are destined to be seen as a threat, are losing touch with children and being childlike, and are emotionally detached and unhealthy. Furthermore, men suffer higher rates of substance abuse (attempts at self-medication to anesthetize oneself), have higher rates of cancer (which is, among other things, anger eating a person from the inside out) and heart dis-ease (a symptom of lack of feeling, lack of expression), and are reporting ever-increasing rates of depression. When we remove ourselves as threats to women and children and when we stop supporting rape culture, then we will also remove ourselves from the cancer ward, the suicide watch, and the need for self-anesthetizing drugs. We will be able to have true, deep friendships with women and men of all ages, of all races, of all sexual orientations.

The threat of rape and harassment makes it difficult for women and men to work together as productively as we could. When we remove men as a threat to women, we will increase our country's productivity and economic output. When men see the benefits that we personally receive from working to stop rape and actively contributing our part, they will see that there is no need for guilt or shame.

This chapter has discussed only the most blatant and most general barriers to men's involvement. There are others, many others. And each of us have our own personal barriers that make doing anti-rape work difficult. We struggle with our shyness, our discomfort with conflict, our lack of self-esteem, or perhaps our fear of being rejected. These are personal issues we all have. But barriers can be overcome. We can find ways around, over, under, or through these barriers—most of which are self-imposed. If we are serious about eliminating men's violence, then we will find a way.

# FIVE

# BEGINNING ANTI-RAPE WORK

BY DEFINITION HUMAN beings have unlimited intelligence, unending creativity, and boundless abilities to love both ourselves and others. Human beings, both male and female, are utterly magnificent! We take up space in the universe; our bodies, our minds, and our souls all take up space, as do all things. Like all things in the universe, we are interwoven in this incredible and beautiful web of life. The choices that I make today, the ways that I act affect not only the rest of my life but also impact the entire universe. The immense specialness of human beings is in our singular and incredible ability to choose how our space within the universe will look. We can and do, consciously or not, choose how we want to express ourselves—and as such, chose consciously *how* to affect the direction and feeling of the universe. Like a web, life has strands that all interconnect and which work in concert to maintain the integrity of the whole. Each strand is necessary for the web to maintain itself. If one strand is "out of place" or moves in some way, the entire system is changed. When looking at a web, we are rarely able to identify all the ways that all the strands interconnect and work together, but we know they do. Our individual lives are the strands in the giant web of life. We can't know exactly the impact of our life will have, or how we're interwoven. But we can know that we are interconnected, and that we do have an impact. None of us can know the impact on the whole of our individual choices, but we can know that there is an impact and to act according to that knowledge. Imagine if each strand of a spider's web could choose its path: that's the ability, power and creativity that we have.

Empowerment comes from recognizing the strength, the beauty, and the innate power of choosing our own path. Empowerment is about recognizing those abilities, and that wisdom to make conscious decisions about the ways that we are going to affect the universe in which we live. Please know that you already influence the universe. Empowerment comes from recognizing that and choosing *how* you want to impact the universe.

Men have the ability to act against rape, and to create a rape-free universe. A great deal of power comes from refusing to live our lives in the ways we've been taught. By making conscious and concrete decisions about how to live our lives, we gain power—true power as defined and first expressed by feminists. Recognizing that we can choose not to play into the myths, lies, and misinformation we've been taught about "being a man" holds great power, *true* power. Men are quite clearly unhappy, and unhealthy. By taking full response-ability for our own happiness and health and making conscious choices about what "being a man" means for us and how to express our masculinity, we are well on our way to becoming empowered.

This new way of "being a man" is not only healthy, but is health*ful*. We can then turn that increased energy outward into the world and work effectively for cleaning up the environment, saving the world economy, and creating a world where justice reigns and peacefulness is the norm.

I want to ask you to reflect for a moment. Stop reading and just sit for a few minutes and imagine a world without rape. Get that picture in your head, and feel it in your heart and soul. Get it, hold onto it, stay with that picture. Now, move that picture onto *our* world, your city, your state, your neighborhood. Imagine a world where your daughter, son, or grandchildren will never have to fear the threat of rape. Finally, move that picture to tomorrow! See waking up tomorrow morning and getting ready for your job, or school, or to do whatever you do tomorrow in a world where there is no more rape! *That* is the world we are striving for and that we deserve to be living, and it is possible and obtainable. It won't be easy, but we most assuredly can get there!

The only way for rape to end—the only way for us to create a world of "gender justice"*—is for us men to act in our full power in ways that interrupt the current system. It is up to men to stop rape. Not only does this mean that each individual man must take the response-ability to stop participating in rape and rape behavior in our own lives but collectively,

---

*John Stoltenberg first coined this phrase.

men must take the personal and public response-ability to end rape in all its forms, which includes confronting rape-supporting attitudes, supporting feminists and other women who are confronting rape, and supporting the survivors of men's sexual violence.

When we are silent about rape, and don't actively work to confront rape-supporting attitudes, and when we continue to act out our male privilege, we act in ways that support the social and political systems in which rape occurs. We are, in effect, supporting rape! Stopping rape requires that we change the ways that we live our personal lives in such a way that directly and publicly confronts the attitudes that support rape. This means challenging ourselves and our friends when we hear racesexism; talking about issues of sexual violence during the dinner discussion of politics and peace; confronting our parent's heterosexism; creating ways to confront rape or sexual harassment in our work places and our classrooms, including when the perpetrator is our brother, friend, or co-worker. In short, we need to create peer pressure among men that doesn't allow rape-supporting behaviors in *any* form to be expressed!

When we hear men making sexist, racist, or heterosexist comments, label what's happening. There's been a rise in recent years of "drug-free zones" all over the country: homes, businesses, neighborhoods, entire towns and cities. Men can create our space as a "harassment-free zone" or "sexism-free zone." Identify your personal space as free from sexism. When sexism invades your space, clean it out—just like when drugs invade a "drug-free zone." Be aware of the subtle and not-so-subtle expressions of rape-supporting behaviors and the ways that they impact *your* life, and don't allow them to occur. Challenge attitudes and behaviors that go on around you all the time! When a man makes a sexist comment, a housemate says something racist, a co-worker supports heterosexism—say something about it. When a movie you're watching celebrates or eroticizes violence against women, write a letter to the producer. When an article in your local paper blames a survivor of rape, write a letter to the editor. Creating a harassment-free zone means demanding that elected officials make a clear statement about what they plan to do to address men's violence *before* they get your vote. It means coming out in a public way to say that you do not support rape!

Another layer of men's work is to take responsibility to ensure that the services assisting the survivors of men's sexual violence continue. Rape crisis centers consistently have difficulty maintaining funding at an adequate level to support the staff and to provide the services that are needed. Because it is due to men's behavior that these services are necessary, men must take responsibility to ensure that these services are adequately funded. Men continue to maintain a virtual stranglehold on funding sources. Not only do men continue to make, on the average, 35 percent more than women, but men also maintain a virtual monopoly on funding sources such as the federal and state governments and private charity organizations. Given this leverage, men must take responsibility to provide funding for these services.

Taking responsibility for men's sexual violence, however, does not include tightening the reins of control around women's lives and defining women's choices. Men frequently respond to the issue of taking responsibility by considering more ways for *women* to limit their behaviors. For example, one of the ways that men generally approach these issues is to work with women: teaching women self-defense skills, becoming involved in escort services, teaching women to shoot a gun, and encouraging women not to walk alone after dark. All of these suggestions may be worthwhile for some women, but for men to make these kinds of suggestions puts men in a position of once again being in control—of defining what women could do that could make them more safe from men's violence. It is not appropriate for men to limit women's possibilities. It is not appropriate for men to consider ways that women should or should not act in response to rape or the threat of rape. Men must take the responsibility for *men's* behavior. The best and most useful way for men to make women safe from men's violence is for us to work to remove the threat. Rather than being "supportive" and finding ways to put more restrictions of women's lives, our time would be better served working with other men. We need to learn how to make sure we're not being offensive, harassing, or abusive and that we are confronting the underlying attitudes that support rape, harassment, and abuse.

In part, rape continues because of men's silence and secrecy. For centuries men have raped with impunity as well as with the backing of legal and judicial power. When men refuse to acknowledge rape behavior, don't listen when women define rape behavior, or refuse to confront other men or themselves when they see rape behavior, men are once again using silence to allow rape to continue. We benefit from the continued existence of rape. Men who rape have buddies, hang out, go to locker rooms, and sit in other men-only arenas. More than likely, they have expressed their rape-supporting attitudes and behavior in other, more "subtle" ways long before the actual rape. That casual remark or joke is an opportunity that men have to challenge those rape-supporting attitudes. Breaking this silence—and thus the tacit support—acts as a powerful tool to deflate rape of some of its power over women.

## HOW WE CAN RESPOND: TAKING A STEP

Beyond confronting rape in men's personal lives, we also are responsible for confronting rape behavior in men's public lives. As discussed earlier, rape is as much a political crime as it is a personal tragedy. As such, men must take the personal responsibility to confront rape as a political act. Confronting the political crime of rape requires that we first define rape as a political act. For a more expansive understanding of this issue, men can begin by listening to women discuss the ways that their lives are limited by rape as a cultural reality.

Malcolm X said about whites:

> Whites who are sincere should organize themselves and figure out strategies to break down the prejudice that exists in white communities. This is where they can function more intelligently, more effectively, and this has never been done.

I think this idea is certainly applicable for men in relation to sexism and rape. We do our best work when we work with other men on creating a rape-free world.

So far, this book has been very heady—very "traditionally male." But I want for this to be more than a cerebral exercise. I want to offer some concrete ideas of actions you can take in your own life, in your community, and in the world to begin effectively confronting rape culture. Please remember that the following suggestions are ideas. Some are based on experience; others are brainstorms that have never been adequately tried. But the one major idea that I want for you to take from reading this book is to take your next step. Whatever step that is, standing where you are will not end men's violence. As James Baldwin said, "The most radical step you can take is your next one."

## GETTING STARTED: ENDING MEN'S VIOLENCE IN YOUR DAILY LIFE

One of the most painful and often most difficult places to begin working to end men's violence is probably one of the most necessary. It is vital that each and every one of us, as men, take a hard and painful look at our behaviors and attitudes to see the ways we support rape culture. This work requires a constant vigilance. It means never quite forgetting that we are men, and that we are granted some privilege based on that. For men of color, gay and bisexual men, younger men, disabled men, and men of other disenfranchised groups, it gets complicated. As a representative of a disenfranchised group, it is important for empowerment and liberation to recognize yourself as part of that community and that set of shared experiences. However, as *men*, even men of a disenfranchised group, we still have privilege based on our gender—privilege that women don't have the luxury of assuming. As such, we can never let ourselves forget that, particularly when relating with women.

Furthermore, we need to look at where on the continuum of sexism we are and in what ways we perpetrate which kinds of sexism, racism, homophobia, age-ism, and other kinds of oppressive behaviors. In order to clean up our behavior, and to become fully empowered, we need to take a completely honest inventory of how we act, the attitudes we hold, and in what ways we act oppressively and abusively. Empowerment requires no less! As in any other kind of honest inventory, it is painful and difficult. But becoming completely empowered makes it all worthwhile.

### Three Questions to Ask Yourself*

To begin, ask yourself a few questions. Ask yourself to remember a time when you've felt like you needed to prove your manhood. Where did that pressure come from? What was going on that you had to prove yourself? What was threatening you and why? What was your image of a "man" at that time? Why did you feel like you needed to prove your manhood? How had you lost your masculinity in that context? Try also to remember on a deeper level. What were you feeling and thinking? Try to remember what your chest was doing, how your breathing felt, what your hands were doing, and how tightly your feet were clenched. How were you able to express yourself at that moment? What did you say and how did you say it? What did you want to say? What did you want to do? What got in the way of you saying or doing what you wanted to say or do—what got in the way of you expressing yourself honestly? And then, how did you go about "proving yourself?" And what happened?

Here's a second question to ponder: How have you acted to intimidate somebody? It can be anybody or any situation—not necessarily related to a sexual experience (although that too would certainly be appropriate). Remember a time when you've tried to make somebody *feel* that you were in a position "over" them. Remember what it felt like, and try to remember what was going on for you at the time. Again, consider the emotions you had, as well as the physical sensations: What were your hands doing, how was your breathing, what was happening in your

---

*Thanks to Margo Adair for assisting me in developing this section.

stomach, how tightly were your feet clenched? What were you thinking and feeling? What happened?

When have you manipulated someone to get what you wanted? When have you used your male-ness, in whatever subtle way, to create a situation in which you got your sexual needs met? Most, if not all of us, have done this regardless of our sexual orientation. You may have to go back a few years (at least back a few years to a point when you can admit to yourself that you did something like that), but the vast majority of us used male privilege when we began dating. Teenagers don't have a whole lot of clear rules for dating—and rules are truly nonexistent for gay youth. We knew that we were supposed to be attached to somebody of the "opposite" sex (or be a "misfit"); that we, as men, were supposed to initiate any interactions; and that we should be having sex with that person (or we wouldn't be a "real man"). But no blue prints were circulated about how to get from here to there. When you add to this confusion the messages that adolescents get from movies, music, videos, and books, then you have a situation set up for acquaintance rape. Most of us probably committed this form of rape. It may not be a prosecutable situation, or even near the law. But seen through the experience of the person with whom we had sex, if they felt forced, pressured, or manipulated, then it becomes closer and closer to rape.

These questions are not an attempt to get you to feel bad about yourself. These questions are an attempt for us as men to take a good look at ourselves. We need to begin looking at just how easy it is to be abusive. It is only by having a clear understanding of the dynamics of sexual abuse that we will be able to begin working towards solutions. It is only when we recognize how common and flagrant these behaviors are that we are in a position to reach other men—not from a higher moral plane, but from a place of being in the same boat, of recognizing the struggle and remembering the difficulty of acknowledging to ourselves that we have hurt people. In this context, the young man at Duke University I described earlier becomes much less of a Neanderthal and much more of a man who is really struggling with his own memories of having hurt women and/or men whom he cared about. When we recognize our own humanity—the good and the not-so-good—we are better able to recognize the humanity of others.

### Learning to Listen to Our Sexual Partners

One of the most obvious ways for us as men to begin taking full responsibility for rape in our personal lives is to listen to the women or men we are sexually involved with when they say no. You need to be explicitly clear about their sexual boundaries, and they need to know that you will respect those boundaries. It really isn't important that we understand why they may be saying no or that we understand the timing of when they choose to say no. The only thing that is important is that they are saying no and that must be respected *absolutely*. Take "no means no" one step further—ask before you touch. Ask the person you are dating if holding hands is okay, if they are comfortable sharing a kiss or a hug, if they want to share sex, if they are comfortable with the ways you are sharing sex.

Women and men who don't want sex don't say no for lots of reasons. For example, this person may be a survivor of sexual abuse or assault. The only way to know if a person with whom we are being intimate is a survivor is if that person chooses to disclose it to us. Coming out is an extremely brave act—particularly coming out to a person they have some positive feelings or attraction for but whom they know rather superficially. Coming out means not only having to deal with a fear of rejection but also having to confront the feelings associated with having been victimized all over again, only now with a person they don't know all that well. It is very difficult, if not impossible, for those who haven't been victimized to understand the impact of the sexually victimizing experience, even when a survivor expresses those feelings.

When survivors start becoming sexual, it can trigger memories of their victimizing experience(s). This is called a "flashback," and, tragically, the survivor remembers more than the intellectual memory. Survivors may remember the physical, the emotional, and the spiritual memory as well, alongside the pain associated with that memory. Many survivors learned that in order to stay alive during the attack(s) they had to freeze and may respond similarly during a flashback. For some survivors, becoming sexual is so terrifying and has been enmeshed with such extremes of violence and domination that they freeze—just as they may have done when they were four and the person forcing sex on them was their father. In a flashback not only do they revert to being four, but the experience reverts to the abusive experience—and the person with whom they are involved stops being their lover and becomes their father.

Given the statistics of sexual abuse of children, it is likely that we have all dated adult survivors of childhood abuse. To ask before we touch offers that person the opportunity to make some conscious decisions about their comfort level with touch and intimacy within a very specific situation. Asking can move the situation from one in which the person is reacting to one where she or he is consciously and actively participating. The end result is that she or he is potentially more able to fully enjoy those experiences. Furthermore, asking permission and establishing a dialogue creates a pattern of being connected and present with our partners. The act of asking in and of itself is certainly important, but the dynamics that asking sets up are truly liberating, and do much to reduce the incidence of rape.

Just because a person may be silent doesn't make the crime any less traumatic, damaging, or hurtful—it does not make it any less a rape. *Silence does not mean yes.* People may be silent for any number of reasons, reasons we don't necessarily need or have the right to know. We need to offer every opportunity for them to voice their needs and to create an environment in which it is okay for them to state their needs.

Regardless of whether the person with whom we are sharing sexually has survived sexual victimization, all people deserve that same level of respect, honesty, and direct communication. The only way to really *know* that we aren't doing something against another person's will and that we aren't forcing them (however "subtle" or "gentle" the force may be) is to ask and hear them say "yes."

It is very difficult to do. We are taught, in our sex-phobic rape culture, that we aren't supposed to talk abut sex. It's a strong taboo that many of us grow up with and internalize deeply! We learn about sex by talking about the "birds and the bees." By the time many of us have had the "sit-down talk" with our parents, we have already gotten so many mixed and confusing messages from the culture about sex and what it is and isn't that we don't even know where to begin, and certainly don't know what questions to ask. We aren't supposed to talk about it in schools. We joke about "doing the nasty" or create some other kind of euphemism to talk about sex. More than any other lesson about sex that we've learned, we've learned to be embarrassed. So to bring up the topic with someone we're dating seems impossible. It's embarrassing, it's scary, it's confusing, and you feel really vulnerable and uncomfortable. This discomfort reinforces the necessity. It is by talking about sex that we will begin losing some of our embarrassment about the topic—and who better to talk about sex with than the person we are or are hoping to share sex with? Not only will this decrease the incidence of rape, it will increase the pleasure of sex.

I know that a lot of you are probably feeling that I am unfairly placing too much responsibility on you. You're very likely asking, "What about their responsibility?!?" First off, this isn't about blame or guilt. Second, this is a person for whom we have some feelings, even if the sexual experience is a purely physical one. When we care about somebody, we care about what's happening for them; we care about making sure they aren't being hurt. Third, I'm talking about men. I'm talking about making sure that we aren't forcing somebody to do something they aren't comfortable with—making sure that we aren't raping. Fourth, we can only take responsibility for ourselves and our actions. We can only take responsibility for reducing the likelihood that we rape. Finally, I'm talking about good sex! The best way to have really good sex is to be with a person who wants to be with you and who is completely and actively involved. *That* is good sex! And that doesn't happen if we are acting "on" our partner, only when we are interacting *with* them.

One long-standing myth of male privilege is the right to touch people whenever we desire, especially the women and children in our lives. A major rationale for that myth is based on women as "property" of men and on the assumption that women in men's lives should succumb to the desires of men. This thinking has often been expanded beyond the limited circle of women directly in the lives of a particular man to include *all* women.

This picture gets further confused when dealing with issues of racism: "Racism has always drawn its strength from its ability to encourage sexual coercion" (Davis, p. 177). White men have a long tradition of controlling and being considered the legal "owners" of women of color. When European men first landed in the Western hemisphere, they assumed the "savagery" of the Native people, and so the right to enslave Native people and sexually victimize Native women. The history of white men raping and otherwise victimizing female slaves is notorious. White men also sexually attacked Latina and Asian women. Part of the right of this sense of ownership included the rights to control their bodies. One of the ways that white men expressed our ownership and dominance was to demand and force sexual relations with women and men of color.

A weapon was to accuse men of color (it was usually the white men, not white women, who made the allegations) of raping white women and use those usually false accusations to attack, beat, kill, and not too infrequently sexually victimize men of color. Another level of the rationale for the ongoing sexual victimizing of women of color has been the creation of an image of women of color as "seductress," as being more animalistic or less than fully human. Therefore, attacking them is not acknowledged as problematic since they don't have human feelings. One of the primary weapons used to maintain the slave system (and the system of white supremacy) was to rape Black women.

The concept that women of color are not completely human has continued throughout our history and continues even to current times. In media images of women, we rarely see women of color, and when we do see them, it is almost always Black women who have very (idealized) white features (small, thin nose; long flowing hair, thin bodies, and small hips), or they fit the white stereotype of what a Black woman is: big, loud, and sexually available. Other women of color appear even more rarely.

This assumption of nonhuman status is probably most clearly demonstrated in pornography. When women of color are photographed in pornography, they are virtually always shown with animals, with chains or whips or other violent imagery, or with more than one male. We who are white know unconsciously about these images and about how they affect our views of women of color. Part of this knowledge is historical, but part of this knowledge comes from today. White men sexually harass and otherwise abuse women of color frequently, and, on the rare occasions that we are actually caught and brought to trial, are even less likely to receive appropriate punishment than we do when we attack white women. The message is clear, and it is learned: Women of color are easier targets and sanctions are less likely. The vast majority of sexual assaults are intraracial (i.e., white men raping white men, Black men raping Black women, etc.). When rapes are interracial, they are overwhelmingly white men raping women or men of color.

Furthermore, men of color do not have the same kinds of power in relation to white women. I'm not saying that men of color do not and have not sexually victimized white women. Rather, because of racism, men of color have not had the same white male rationale that sees white women as their "property"—and certainly not the same white male perspective on women of color. Men of color have been kept dispossessed in the hierarchy of white supremacy. Despite active resistance, they have been the ones who have been bought and sold, beaten and killed with impunity along with their sisters of color. They have not been in a position of power and domination over white women and so have been unable to develop an ownership mentality. Again, this is not to say that some men of color don't rape, or that some don't have feel the sense of entitlement over all women (including white women) that white men have. But the dynamics are different and do need to be taken into account with any analysis of sexual violence and when working to stop rape.

*More Steps to Take*

Other ways of men can take responsibility in their personal lives include:

- ensuring that survivor service organizations have the funding to stay open
- actively and caringly supporting rape survivors

- participating equally in housework and child care
- respecting women's space
- not viewing pornography
- not interrupting women
- talking with other men about these issues
- confronting expressions of sexism
- exposing the connections between sexism, racism, heterosexism, and other expressions of oppression in the ways they all support rape culture

As men, we need to be forever aware of our male privilege, and the ways we act out this privilege. For example, beginning in the summer and fall of 1990, I participated in the development of the Violence Against Women Act filed by Senator Joe Biden and (then) Representative Barbara Boxer. I was frequently one of the only men in the room when the task group organized by the NOW Legal Defense and Education Fund would meet. During those at times heated discussions with representatives from civil rights and women's rights organizations, I needed to always remember the ways that gender politics were getting played out. I had to be constantly vigilant to the ways I acted out my male privilege and what impact my "acting up" was having on the dynamics of what was going on in the room. At times it was even stated I was listened to differently because I am a man. It was most clear when members of Congress interacted more directly with me, even when I was saying less. In one rather extreme example, a male aide talked almost exclusively to me throughout the entire meeting and rarely looked at the women in the room. This isn't to say that I needed to stifle myself; rather, it is to say that I need to be aware constantly of expressions of male privilege (mine and others) and the ways they impact what is happening. Acting out male privilege is one form of supporting rape.

## LISTENING AND READING

One method for beginning and sustaining this self-examination and self-discovery is through listening to women, and through reading whatever we can get our hands on that relates to any of these topics. We have to start with definitions, and we have to come to a clear understandings *for ourselves* of these issues. Once we have developed an understanding of the definitions and the issues surrounding men's violence, we have taken a gigantic step toward taking action. It is much easier to start from a perspective of clarity and knowledge than from uncertainty and ignorance. As you begin, learn all you can about the issues. As you became more knowledgeable, you begin examining ways that you could become more active. As you know more, you start to care more. Additionally, as you know more, you become better at identifying possible solutions.

When talking and listening with others on these issues, talk with more than your mouth and listen with more than your ears. Men are trained to become "experts." We are taught to learn what there is to learn and then be able to spit out *the* answers—the more the better. Part of the tragedy of this kind of training is that many of us have learned to do most of our listening through the left half of our brains. The information that comes through to us is limited to very logical, rational, systematic, mathematical kinds of information. As a result, we miss a lot.

Men need to begin learning new ways to listen, as well as learning new ways to talk and to learn. Part of that process means turning on and into our hearts as well as our minds. It means listening with our feelings and hearing another person's feelings as they explain their views. Basically, we must reconnect with our intuitive sides. For example—what feelings are coming up for you right now as you read these words? Where are your hands—and in what position? What are your feet doing? How's your breathing? How fast is your heart beating? How high and tight are your shoulders? These kinds of observations are a part of the process. To listen and learn with more than our mouths requires a willingness to check in with ourselves and examine the feelings and thoughts being triggered by the process around us.

Similarly, men need to be conscious of the way we talk with others to take into account how our words and delivery affect those who are listening. It is one thing to say what needs to be said, but it is another to say that in a way that is mindful of where and who the listeners are.

We need to learn to truly listen for a variety of reasons. First, men are taught to talk. One of the more common male control patterns is to control the conversation. We express this control pattern with women by interrupting, by talking over or past women, by ignoring women, or by clarifying what women have to say. By listening carefully to what women have to say, we can begin breaking one of our oppressive patterns. We can also begin creating a new vision of male-female interactions.

Second, and just as important, we can learn something when we take the time to shut up and listen. We can learn about the impact of rape culture on women's daily lives: the pain, rage, frustration, and despair. Sometimes, hearing these kinds of revelations is the best teacher. I have to offer a warning here—at times those feelings are very raw for women. Talking about the ways we are oppressed and the impacts of that oppression on our personal lives with a member of the oppressor class can touch some very deep and raw nerves. And sometimes women use this opportunity to do some emotional venting. We need to learn how to hear what is being said without becoming defensive, or blowing off what is said as "too emotional."

For some of us, getting blasted is the only way to "blast" through the defensiveness and denial we have built up. For example, a couple of years ago, I was invited to Atlanta to do some organizing and speaking on issues of rape and racism in response to an increase in rape and racism there. Various interesting and confrontational actions took place during the week I was there. Upon my return, a couple of women friends were very angry with me for "stirring things up and leaving." They were quite angry and explicitly told me how my short time there, organizing and going home, was yet another example of my white and male privilege. The people I had worked with had to stay in Atlanta and deal with whatever trouble was left, while I was safely away. Initially, my defenses were very strong and I defended what I had done, and charged my friends with being unfair, urging them to ask the people in Atlanta what they thought. This only fueled their anger.

Finally, I came to understand their concerns. They were right, it was an example of white and male privilege. I was asked to come to Atlanta precisely because I am white and male, and because I speak on these issues. Plenty of women of color are much more articulate than I, and some of them live in the Atlanta area. My trip was also an example of privilege in that I had the privilege to come back home when the heat got too intense. I didn't have to stay and deal with the ramifications like the local organizers did. I don't think that because it exemplified white and male privilege the value of what we did there is necessarily lessened. However, I need to be aware of the subtle (and perhaps not so subtle) ways that I express my privilege—and be willing to identify it, label it and confront it. It is by understanding more clearly how all of us can get caught in the traps of patriarchy that we increase our abilities to destroy it.

The only way I was able to hear what they said was because they kept after me. Had they tried a more gentle approach, I probably would not have been aware of my defensiveness, much less been willing to acknowledge and own the concerns they raised. In that situation, I needed them to confront me as strongly and directly as they did so I could get through my own denial. Further, I needed to hear their anger at me. I needed to hear (with more than my ears) the ways that my expressing white-male privilege hurt and angered them. When I realized the cost to them and to our relationship, my commitment deepened.

Patriarchy cannot handle women and men (or white people and people of color, or queers and heterosexuals) working effectively together. As a result, patriarchy will do anything in its power to maintain the status quo, mostly through helping us distrust or devalue each other. Sometimes that gets played out in our interpersonal relationships and sabotages the possibility of our working well together. I've been in situations where I wasn't able to continue working with a particular woman; rather than being ethical and appropriate, I shut down and acted in ways that undermined our ability to work together to really make a difference. I remember an occasion where a woman and I were both trainers in a high school. We offered a day-long workshop with seven classes on sexual and gender harassment. It became very clear very quickly that she and I had some very different perspectives on the issues. Rather than talk about that directly, honestly, or ethically, I chose to offer my perspective in spite of her presence. The day went okay—in fact, it went fairly well—in spite of me. But I often think how much better it could have been had I taken the initiative to clarify our messages to the students. Furthermore, think how important it would have been for those young people to see a man and a woman disagree on these kinds of issues in an ethical and respectful manner.

## SHARING: THE IMPORTANCE OF A SUPPORT NETWORK

Living an anti-rape lifestyle is just plain hard: the self-examination, your new role as the "heavy" at your friends' parties, the speaking, the fund-raising, the sight of rape culture everywhere. This lifestyle, whatever form it may take, cannot be lived effectively in a vacuum—it's too hard and demanding. As I've discussed, a sense of isolation occurs when living an anti-rape lifestyle. Attempting to live this kind of life in a isolation only sets you up for burnout, and severely reduces your ability to do what you need to do. When I first began, working and living against men's violence in Texas, the only men I knew who were involved were hundreds of miles away. As such, I was very isolated. I didn't believe that the men who were my friends would or could understand what was happening to me, which left me feeling very lonely and interrupted my abilities to do what I needed to do. When I moved to Washington, DC, I discovered a men's group (DC Men Against Rape) who gathered regularly and discussed being men against rape. I found that other men could understand what I was going through and be supportive. And I could find ways to articulate my process.

As a result, I discovered that I had exponentially more energy, more commitment, and more creativity for doing anti-rape work.

At another level, my difficulty in continuing to do this work became compounded as I began seeing many of the behaviors exhibited by men who batter in my dormmates and in myself. As I started to really understand that it was not "those" men who caused the women they cared for to run to the shelter, but rather it was the men I lived with as well as cared about, I saw the man in the mirror. I began to see the ways that we (I include myself in this) interacted with the women on campus in a different light. The slurs we would make about their bodies and bodily functions were the same slurs I heard from men calling the shelter to try to find their wives and explaining that "the bitch had it coming." I saw men I respected (and myself) "jokingly" raise our hands to the women we were dating—the same way "those" men raised their hands in a menacing manner to intimidate their girlfriends. I listened to the ways that we made gross generalized comments about all women, and particularly generalizations about certain kinds of women. I heard anew as we harassed the cheerleaders, the female basketball players, and the college women on the street. I started to see the ways that all of us act out the same basic behaviors that many men take to the "not-so-extreme" extreme of battering, abuse, or rape.

I urge that you do the same thing. Find or create a men's group with whom you can talk about these issues. Share what you are going through with the people in your life. They may not understand; they may force you to become more articulate in describing what you're confronting and dealing with. In retrospect, I was not only selling my friends short, but I was also selling myself short: perhaps they could have understood, or I could have found a way to make it clear. Probably, value would have come from talking with other men regardless of how articulate I was, or their ability to understand what I was trying to say. Even though I may not have been validated in the same way that DC Men Against Rape affirmed me, I may have discovered some support and some deep and considerate thinking on their part about this struggle. Further, I would have most likely found that I wasn't the only one. It's a safe bet that other men living in that dorm were also having a hard time with a lot of the same questions I began to ask: What does it mean to "be a man"? How do I share with women? What kind of lover do I want to be? The process of sharing is so necessary.

You will probably feel incredibly isolated by searching for answers to these questions; to attempt this process in a state of isolation seems almost self-abusive. Talk with your partner and your friends about the issues this book brings up for you. Talk with them, particularly new friends, about what kinds of touching they do and don't like. Begin discovering for yourself what kinds of touching you do and don't like. Talk with your friends about what situations make them uncomfortable. Ask for feedback, for critiques. And allow yourself to be open to whatever comes back, as well as whatever feelings arise for you. I encourage you to listen to what is said, and to allow yourself time to respond to what they offer. I would offer a warning about responding too quickly, and too intelligently. If people are brave and loving enough to offer critiques of you, then listen. You don't necessarily have to agree with what they say, but do listen, and listen carefully. The stronger your reaction, the greater the likelihood that they may be getting "close to home."

Describe with your friends, male and female, what it is like for you to read this book. When asked "Read any good books lately?" try describing the process you experienced as you read this book in addition to the content. Talk from your heart as well as from your head. Talk with an awareness from your gut, and what is happening there as well. It may seem overwhelming to try and do all of this at once—and it probably is to some extent. But remember, this is all a process, and you will learn and become more competent as you gain experience and practice. Allow yourself to move, allow yourself to "fail," and allow yourself to grow.

# SIX

# EMPOWERMENT
## Men Taking Action

Every *man* must decide whether he will walk in the light of creative altruism or the darkness of destructive selfishness. This is the judgement. Life's most persistent and urgent question is *what are you doing for others?*

—Martin Luther King, Jr., 1962 (emphasis added)

READING AND WRITING about issues of men's sexism and sexist violence, supporting and challenging ourselves and each other in a respectful environment, offering support for survivors, and exposing the connections between rape and other forms of oppression are all necessary, but that is not enough. Men must begin taking action, in whatever form that may take. The focus of this book is what men can do to stop rape. Men can do much in our personal lives. But my main goal is to encourage more men to organize and become active in their communities to stop rape. More than anything else, I hope that this book acts as a springboard for the development of Men Against Rape groups in every community.

Men have access to the boardrooms, the classrooms, the locker rooms, the bars, to any and all of the places where men congregate. We can use those opportunities creatively to educate. Men tend to listen more and better to men than we do to women. If you are supportive of women and are committed to ending men's violent behaviors, then it is incumbent on you to "break the silence to end men's violence" (the slogan of BrotherPeace, a project of the Ending Men's Violence Network)—it's incumbent upon you to ACT! The only way that men will begin responding appropriately to issues of men's violence and begin working towards a more peaceful world is by men putting action on our agendas.

As men, we must band together and publicly call for an end to male violence, adequate support for programs providing services for survivors, appropriate educational programming, safer streets, and better child care. We must tear the pornographic pictures off the locker doors, from the hallways, and from our minds. We must interrupt men's sexism and confront harassment by other men. When men create peer pressure to interrupt rape-supporting behaviors on a consistent and ongoing basis, then we will begin to see a reduction in rape. The only way to get there from here is one step at a time. Men need to start taking steps—and making tracks—towards a rape-free world.

This chapter will focus on what men can do, and how men can organize in our own communities in a variety of ways to end men's violence. It also offers several examples of events that can lend themselves to a forum on men's violence which can interrupt the patterns of victimization.

## NONVIOLENCE

A commitment to nonviolence is an absolute necessity for any man doing work against men's violence and oppression. When we act, it is essential that we be grounded in a solid understanding of nonviolence. Nonviolence is more than just the absence of violence—nonviolence is the presence of justice. Men acting without a commitment to nonviolence is no different than men acting in any other form. And, as is true with most issues but particularly in ending men's violence, the end cannot be separated from the means. In order to get to a rape-free world, we must begin acting rape-free lives. That *requires* a commitment to nonviolence.

Nonviolence begins with an understanding, an acceptance, and a recognition of each person's inherent humanity and, thus, each person's inherent right to be treated with complete dignity and respect. *Each person!* At the core of violence is a process of stripping a layer of a person's humanity away. It's part of the militaristic mindset that is so much a part of all of us. You learn to define the "enemy," dehumanize them, and hold rigidly to the concept of "them" as "enemy." As a result, it becomes easier to live with yourself when you try to kill them (in fact, it is impossible to kill them without going through a similar process). Using slurs to describe people is a part of the process of stripping their humanity from them, so that they no longer deserve the dignity and respect that all human beings are due. For example, think of a time when you're driving and you get cut off. If you're anything like me, and a majority of drivers, you scream something like "YOU *&%$#@*%*# PIG!!!"—which separates him (say it's a him) from his humanity. From there, you use the fact that he is now a "*$%* ^&&*# PIG" to justify further fueling your anger, and gun your engine to go "get him"—flipping him off or cutting him off in return. Since you have successfully dissociated (both him and yourself) from your respective humanity, you can justify doing to him what he did to you.

That's a simple example, but the process is the same. When we think of men who harass, use pornography, are sexist, or who rape as inhuman, "monsters" or "animals", we successfully cut them off from their humanity and not only justify murdering them but also separate them from us. We're not like them, after all, so obviously we're not sexist, or the "sexism we do isn't as bad as what they did."

Barbara Deming pointed out the virtues of nonviolence this way:

> Nonviolent confrontation is the only confrontation that allows us to respond realistically to such complexity. In this form of struggle, we address ourselves both to that which we refuse to accept from others, and that which we have in common with them—however much or little that may be. (From McAllister, *Reweaving the Web of Life: Feminism and Nonviolence*, p. 12)

By using nonviolence, we are able to identify the ways that we are like the men who are overtly abusive while at the same time confronting their behavior. This is the only hope of effectively reaching out to them so that they might change.

When doing any action, it is important to stay grounded in these principles. When doing public events, people will respond in many different ways. As long as we stay committed to "reaching one hand out in justice" we increase our ability to actually touch that person. At one event in Washington, DC, an enraged (and probably intoxicated) man began approaching the podium, making abusive comments and asking the speaker to "meet him later." I went over to talk with him, and as he saw me approach, he squared off to meet me, assuming I was coming over to fight him. I backed off a bit, explaining that I just came over to talk—that he seemed angry and agitated and that I didn't want him to continue to interrupt the program. He then directed his anger toward me, but he immediately dropped his hands and unclenched his fists. As he continued to talk, he became less agitated and angry. Had I not allowed him to have his humanity by either ignoring him or attempting to "shut him up!" I would have only been successful at increasing his agitation. By responding in a nonviolent manner that recognized his humanity (by entering into a dialogue even when confronting his interruption), we (he and I—after all, he actually did most of the work) were able to reduce the tension and abusiveness of the situation.

Does a commitment to nonviolence necessarily mean that we are opposed to violence at all times? Frankly, that depends on which nonviolent theorist or activist you agree with. I don't think so: Mahatma Gandhi said that it is "better to resist violently than to submit but it is best of all to resist nonviolently." Violence may always have to be considered an option, for instance when violence has been an ongoing weapon of systematic oppression. For example, my commitment to nonviolence does not mean that I would oppose Blacks in South Africa fighting back against their oppression, or that I condemn battered women who kill the men who abuse them, or that I oppose women or children learning to shoot and get guns in order to protect themselves from men who rape. All of those situations concern and scare me, and I hope they don't have to occur, but it is not my place, coming from a position of privilege, to limit the options that abused or oppressed people have for fighting back.

As men, we are not a dispossessed or oppressed people. Gay and bisexual men are oppressed for being gay or bi; men of color are oppressed for being of color; but men are not oppressed. As such, our use of violence is coming from a very different context than the violence of people who have been oppressed. While I would never limit the already-too-few options of liberation that oppressed peoples have at their disposal, I will always limit the use of violence by men who *do* have other tools at our disposal. Men don't have to use violence to stop rape.

More than a behavior, nonviolence is a state of mind and being that is incorporated into every aspect of your life. If you choose to get more active, then nonviolence can be utilized in an ongoing way—regardless of the kind of activism you choose. Nonviolence can be used when lobbying Congress or your county council; it can be used during educational programs at a high school or at a training at a local business, in a men's reading and discussion group or in any other setting. Coming to whatever form of activism you choose from a perspective of nonviolence simply means *always* recognizing and celebrating the humanity of the people with whom you interact. As such, it means thinking about every encounter as an interaction—the point of which is not to "win" but to engage. It means remembering that you may have as much to learn from the other person as they have to learn from you. It means disengaging from the competitive mindset so common in our thinking, and reengaging from a place of mutual respect. Even when you walk into a hostile environment, you can enter respecting the people you are interacting with, and yourself; they can't help but respect you as well. Nonviolence also reminds us that there is always more than one way to confront rape-supporting behaviors and to encourage a rape-free environment. Nonviolence encourages creativity.

Nonviolence gives us a channel through which to direct our energies, an outlet for our anger. Most of us feel deeply and profoundly angry. We're angry that so many women are victimized, that so many women in our lives have been victimized, that men continue to be so hard to reach, that rape and violence continue to increase despite our efforts, and that we've been set up to be abusive and seen as a threat. This anger can feel overwhelming and can exacerbate burnout unless we provide opportunities to release that anger. Nonviolent activism gives us those opportunities. By taking direct action to confront the situation in a way that is loud, proud, humane, and nonthreatening, we create an opportunity to release a part of that anger.

Activism too is a mindset more than a behavior. Being "active" simply means *thinking* actively about the situation and the issues. An activist is simply a person who examines and dissects what is happening, looks at various ways to interrupt the process, and engages in the way that seems most appropriate. An activist is someone who responds. By reading right now, you are being active—particularly if you are actively engaged in thinking about what you're reading. Activism is recognizing that you have an ability to respond to a situation, and acting based on that ability. Activism, in short, is acting out empowerment. It isn't necessarily organizing marches or demonstrations or risking arrest in civil disobedience. Activism just means responding actively.

## EDUCATIONAL ACTIVISM

Education is an invaluable tool for creating change. By publicly breaking the silence, we express our support of women, disenfranchised men, and the work that has been done for centuries by feminists as well as for men in general. We also publicly support an end to men's violence and join our voices to the chorus of women who have been shouting for lifetimes. Finally, education offers information, and an example of how people can take action in their own lives.

Education is a process of learning new skills and new ways of looking at the world: bell hooks teaches us, "Education as the practice of freedom." Education teaches the critical-thinking skills men need in order to reevaluate the world and begin to change it. Educating men about rape consists of offering the thoughts that are offered here, and creating an opportunity for them to integrate this thinking into their very souls. Paulo Freire writes about the "integrated person as subject...[where] integration results from the capacity to adapt oneself to reality plus the critical capacity to make choices and transform that reality." As men we can critically examine and transform the world we live in, the definition of masculinity, and the ways that we all support rape culture. That is a first step in personal empowerment and political liberation.

Education can take any number of forms. For my purposes here, I will primarily discuss doing verbal educating in workshops with small groups, while out with friends, and when confronting rape-supporting behaviors or attitudes. One mind shift that may help in doing anti-rape educating is to think of every interaction as an educational opportunity for both the other person(s), and for you. When we are on the subway and someone asks us about a button that we're wearing, that becomes an educational program—for the person we're talking with, as well as for the handful of people who are in our immediate vicinity. Educational opportunities do not have to be formal programs. The only difference between an informal educational program and a formal one is the level of structure. The information and skills are basically the same.

### How Do I Talk with Men About Men's Sexual Violence?

First off, you already know how to talk with men. You already have conversations and engage in "educational forums" with the men in your life. When you sit around after the ballgame discussing the highlights and espousing your views about who made the best plays and why, that's education. When you sit around the dinner table talking about the candidates running for this or that office; when you take a walk to resolve the conflict you're having with a friend—all of these are educational forums. You don't need any special skills to talk to men about sexual violence. You may reply that sexual violence is a bit more challenging and difficult than talking about a sports event, which is certainly true. But you also know how to bring up difficult topics with your friends, colleagues, fellow students, and co-workers; you've done it. I don't want to minimize doing anti-rape educating, but it need not seem daunting or overwhelming.

The best way to talk with men about sexual violence is by being honest about what you know, what you feel, and what you think. If you don't know something, say so. Your responsibility is not to convince anybody but to create an opportunity for men to think *hard* about these difficult and complex issues. Hopefully, they will choose to change their attitudes as a result, but that decision is theirs to make. The best you can do is to offer information.

Perhaps one of the most basic questions that needs to be asked is, "What gets in the way of talking to men?" When you are able to articulate for yourself why you hesitate bringing up sexual violence with your friends, or putting it on the agenda for a staff meeting, you'll be much closer to effectively talking with men about rape.

Not all men are alike, and you won't be able to talk to all men in the same way. Know who you are and acknowledge the perspective you are speaking from, but also know and acknowledge whom you're talking with. Again, you already know that you talk differently with different men: you talk differently with your father than you do with your friends than you do with your co-workers. Take this same understanding into talking about issues of men's violence—and ending men's violence. *Think*, in an active way, about the men you are trying to reach and how to best reach them.

In more structured settings, a few suggestions about talking with men may be helpful. First off, it's important to know that there are different forms of presentations. Each of these requires somewhat different skills. For example, speaking to a large audience is very different than offering a training program which is very different from giving an interview for the media. You may not have the experience or the comfort level, but you *do* have the skills to speak—even in formal settings. It isn't as different from any other kind of speaking as it's made out to be.

One key question that often comes up is, "How do I get opportunities to offer formal presentations?" It helps if you are attached to an organization, such as a Men Against Rape group. From there, begin calling friends or contacts you have in schools, churches, clubs that you belong to, or neighborhood groups. Use whatever format you have at your disposal. Schools, particularly high schools, are often receptive to speakers on these topics. Contact the counseling department or a relevant class such as home economics, English, family life, sex education, or social studies. For your own development as a speaker, it's helpful to start where you are most comfortable. If you start with the organizations you belong to, as your expertise grows so too will your reputation.

Regardless of the format, remember that not everybody is going to stay calm. Sexual violence is an incredibly difficult, painful, enraging, sad, frustrating topic. When honest discussions of these issues occur and people remain calm, then we are not reaching the heart of the matter and we aren't creating an honest dialogue. Men need to get into our hearts and become aware of and express our feelings if we are to have any hope of ever ending men's sexual violence! It is not our purpose to make men feel good or comfortable about rape, rather, our purpose is to create an opportunity for men to honestly discuss and deal with these issues. I prefer discussions that are lively and heated, in which the men are "swinging from the rafters," for that means they are responding in a very real way—perhaps for the very first time—to sexual violence. And that response is a beginning to an appropriate response.

Whenever discussing issues of rape and responsibility with men, two of the most frequent responses are guilt and defensiveness. Men tend to dismiss the message as well as the messenger. This can be expressed in any number of ways, from rather benign to downright cruel. If you can establish a connection between yourself and the participants, they will be much less likely to act in dismissive ways.

Responding to either the guilt or the dismissal is best accomplished by continually restating the obvious, since reacting usually leads to escalation. Remember that you are there to educate and sensitize men on the issue of rape and motivate men to take action to stop rape behavior. Follow through by sticking to your agenda; allow for fluctuation that may have to occur, but not sabotage. If you feel the latter is what is happening, it probably is. First acknowledge the feelings expressed ("It sounds like you feel frustrated and blamed"). Label the behavior for what it is ("I believe you're sabotaging the discussion and am asking you to please stop." Or "You may be angry and frustrated, and we can talk about that further, but I won't allow this discussion to be derailed.") Then restate your points ("This is not about blame or guilt—it's about response-ability. All men benefit because some men choose to use their penises as a weapon. Because all men benefit and receive privilege from rape, all men have a response-ability to work to stop rape."). It can also be helpful to honestly state that they may indeed feel ashamed and blamed; however, the ownership of those feelings needs to be given back where they belong, to the person feeling them. ("I understand that you feel blamed and defensive. But I have nowhere stated that men are bad or wrong. If you feel blamed, those feelings are coming from you, not me.")

Depending on your own style and comfort level, it may be helpful to prepare a loose outline with opportunities for group participation and input. Make sure you have key points that you want to emphasize throughout the discussion. Any and all points that come up during the discussion are important, related, and valuable. However, it is helpful for your own mental health and sense of stability to have a clear idea about which specific issues you want to address. The more you learn about these issues, the more you'll understand the complexity, and as your skills develop, so will your ability to ensure that certain points get covered.

Encourage discussion by asking questions of the group, and create opportunities for them to come up with the points that you want to see emphasized. In discussion format (which I strongly recommend), your role becomes one of facilitator—to guide the discussion and boil down the points into two or three "bite-size" pieces. People tend to learn better when they are given the chance to come up with the answers than when they are told them. For example, when talking about the more subtle forms of sexism and their support of sexual violence, use an example from your own history, and ask the participants to do the same.

I often refer to the privilege I receive in speaking all over the country. I have the opportunity to travel, to meet people, to engage in ideas and learn a great deal from people working on the front lines in a wide variety of settings. But a piece of the privilege is white male privilege. I'm asked to speak not only because what I have to say is valuable but also because I'm a white man who's saying these things. My taking advantage of those opportunities, and accepting payment for those opportunities, is a way that I take advantage of white male privilege and thus support a system in which men are valued more than women. This example may be an overstatement in that I focus most of my work with men—and there aren't a whole lot of women who do what I do. But a piece of male privilege is still floating around. Working to eliminate sexism but taking advantage of male privilege in the process is a contradiction. Yet much of what we do is contradictions. We need to be willing to do what we do acknowledging the contradictions. As Maxine Hong Kingston said, "[I] learn[ed] to make my mind large, as large as the universe is large, so that there [was] room for paradoxes."

People have about a seven- to ten-minute attention span when listening to a presentation. Given that, any presentation should allow participants to be comfortable with the process, be sure to schedule breaks, shifts of focus, exercises, or some other natural change in the flow of the presentation every ten minutes or so. In this way, you increase the likelihood that the participants will stay with you throughout the discussion.

Be sensitive to differences of culture, race, and sexual orientation. In any room, several participants are likely to be gay or bisexual. As such, all discussions should be developed with that awareness and with a consciousness of heterosexist assumptions. Some of the men may have been victimized during gay-bashing attacks, sexually assaulted by strangers, or victimized by acquaintance rape in gay relationships. Create a discussion that is as all-inclusive as possible.

When white men and men of color discuss issues of rape, it is important to acknowledge the ways that lies about rape have been used by white people to continue to oppress, dominate, and violate people of color. These lies depict men of color as forever "lying in wait" for a white woman to rape. A second lie portrays women of color as more appropriate rape targets than white women. This history is most easily seen in the relations of white and Black people; however, similar patterns were and are true between whites and other populations of color as well. Rape has been traditionally defined as a "white problem" within many communities of color. It is essential that white presenters be aware of this as we develop and offer presentations.

## Preparing Presentations for Different Formats

Know the format of the presentation, including the size and makeup of the audience (age, race, gender, sexual orientation, religion), the kind of presentation they expect, and the amount of time you have for the presentation. Regardless of the kind of presentation, there are probably going to be points that you miss, or that you won't have time to go over adequately. As I've discussed, men's sexual violence is incredibly complicated. You can't cover it all. The point of a presentation is not to offer the definitive discussion on sexual violence, but rather to offer men an opportunity to look closely at issues of men's sexual violence and to take responsibility for it. Again, we come back to the need to clarify the key points that you want to make with the presentation and to ensure that those points get made. As always, allow room for flexibility based on the audience.

Clarifying your key points is particularly necessary whenever working with the media. You will have only a very few seconds—moments at best—to make *any* point when working with the media, who tend to take only a very small piece of what you said and often misrepresent that. What are the two points that are *most* important for you to make? Answer whatever questions the media pose in such a way that your points come across. For example, whenever I work with the media, I tend to focus almost exclusively on the "men's response-ability rap"—that men rape, the only way rape will stop is for men to stop raping, and that means that the so-called bad men have to stop raping, and the so-called good men need to stop being silent. I don't say a whole lot more, and whenever they ask a question, I twist my answer to include that statement.

Approach the media cautiously, and include a feminist spokesperson whenever you are given attention. It is very easy to be enamored by the lights and seeing your name in print. But whatever we've learned about these issues has been because of what feminists have taught us. And, bottom line, this is about the lives of women. Women survivors and feminists representing them need to share access to the media that you may be able to create or are given for yourself.

Getting to the media is always a difficulty, but is substantially easier in smaller media markets. For example, writing a letter to the editor or an op-ed piece is one of the best ways to use the media to your advantage. It is very seductive to write something for a major metropolitan newspaper to reach a larger number of people, but a great deal of value also exists in writing articles for and working with smaller and specialty papers: the gay, feminist, Black or Hispanic papers as well as neighborhood and community papers. The chances that those papers will print an article or letter is much greater.

Attempting to get the media to an event that you are organizing is always a challenge, and depends on what else occurs on that day. One event that I organized happened on the same day that President Bush ordered troops into Panama; obviously, we didn't get a whole lot of media coverage on that day. It helps if you can create a relationship with the media people you work with. All media outlets have staff who make decisions about which stories to cover, and a relationship with those people increases the likelihood of media attention. Another possible outlet is cable television stations, which not only look for stories and issues to address but also look for people who are willing to run series. It isn't too challenging to host a talk show through your local cable radio or TV station and air these issues from a variety of perspectives.

Regardless of what you are able to do in terms of creating opportunities to reach male audiences, at times you will probably feel like a complete and utter failure. There will be times when you feel that nothing was accomplished, and that there was no benefit to having done this or that particular event. But keep in mind that you created an opportunity for men to talk about some issues that men rarely talk honestly and openly about. That in and of itself is a success. And it was because of you that the issues were raised in that particular format, and that the issues were raised from the perspective of victim/survivor advocates. That, by definition, is a success. It is also true that you might want more to happen. I am not suggesting that we be satisfied, but we need not be too hard on ourselves.

### Preparing for a Mixed-Gender Audience

Several specific issues should be watched when preparing a discussion for a mixed-gender group. The dynamics are different than in men-only discussions, and the framework for the topic changes.

First, whenever presenting to a mixed-gender audience try to have mixed-gender presenters. (I also urge you to have teams of interracial presentors). It is important that women hear about women's experiences from women, not from men. We may become experts on men and rape, or on perpetrating rape, but we have no business talking to women about what women should know about sexual assault. Many women have the expertise on these kinds of issues, and we need to be working closely with them so that when the opportunities to speak at mixed-gender events arise, we know who to call. This is also an opportunity to model men and women working side by side on these issues.

The dynamics that arise during mixed-gender discussions are different than those in men-only groups. Men in mixed-gender audiences generally aren't as verbal as men in a male-only audience. Men very quickly get a sense of the kinds of answers that will "score the most points" with the women in the room. Men want to look and sound good. That means that men tend to be quiet rather than ask something that could be inappropriate or that identifies us as being "one of those guys." As a facilitator, it is valuable to notice and perhaps acknowledge that dynamic.

It is not at all uncommon for women to disclose their past histories of being victimized. This may be the first time that they've told anyone, and this can obviously be very emotional. Men don't often know how to respond and tend to be overwhelmed by our own feelings at seeing a woman that we may be friends with, work with, or study with discussing their deep hurt—perhaps by men that we know. The person sharing their story may not be very emotional or distraught. They may be sharing it as a "point of information" for the other participants (the survivor may have done enough healing that it isn't traumatic to share, or they might recognize the unlikelihood for support in that setting and so intellectualize the experience to keep the feelings at bay). Regardless, it's difficult for men to be verbal at these times. People, particularly survivors, tend to be very good at taking care of themselves, tend to know when they are in a supportive environment, and where they can go to get any support needed. As such, you don't need to be overly concerned with being able to respond to survivors who disclose—even if they begin crying. However, it is important to be aware of the likelihood and prepared for it happening. Check in with them and see if they need or want anything, thank them and appreciate them for their courage in sharing their story. If they don't ask for support, then gently move on: trust them to be able to meet their needs.

Furthermore, this kind of presentation risks touching memories long buried for some of the participants. It isn't uncommon for women, and occasionally men, to come out with their abuse experiences, and it very well may be the first time they've ever disclosed. This setting is also probably the first time survivors have heard men talk about men taking full responsibility for sexual violence, which can also trigger some intense emotional responses. As presenters, we must walk a careful line, since the workshop forum is not a therapy or support group—and cannot be made into one. At the same time, survivors may need to talk about what they experienced, and it is often very good for men to hear survivors talk about these experiences. Survivors may also come up to you after the presentation to talk or talk more, seeing you as a supportive and caring person. If you don't feel prepared or comfortable responding to them, then have the number of the local rape crisis center to refer them to.

Issues of gender politics *will* get played out during the presentation in numerous ways. Men flirt with female participants; men interrupt women or clarify what women say; and male participants talk to the male presenter, perhaps entirely dismissing the female presenter. Be aware of these issues and how they are acted out. Notice the ways gender lines may get drawn. How are the men and women generally responding to the questions? How and where are they sitting? Which gender is having the side discussions during the presentation? These are important questions to ask and may be valuable to point out.

Finally, it is important to clarify your goals, being as specific and concrete as you can. Working with a mixed-gender audience raises different issues than working with an audience of men. Neither is necessarily better or worse; they are just different. Mixed-gender audiences offer premier opportunities for men to actually listen to women, and women to men, about the impact of men's sexual violence. Men rarely have such an opportunity, so it's often a good experience for them to go through—regardless of the specific outcome. However, men are often not as involved, engaged, or honest when women are in the room.

You want men to listen, but you also want men to participate. This is a thin line to try to walk. It's rather common for men to get very quiet—and it's hard to know what men are thinking and feeling, and how they are responding to what's happening when they are quiet. One way to negotiate this dynamic is to try to focus on issues of men listening to women and really hearing what they say. Have them react not just to the words but to the feelings underneath. Use their silence as a part of the workshop and encourage them to respond.

## THE QUESTION OF ACCOUNTABILITY

All of us are accountable. We account to somebody or some group as well as to ourselves for what we do and how we do it. We account for our actions, our beliefs, and our values. When we offer educational programs, we need to be explicitly accountable to the women, children, and men whose lives are most directly affected by the work that we do, and whose lives we claim to be working to improve. Doing anti-rape education means that we are accountable to survivors of sexual violence, and to feminist women and groups who are working for and with survivors. Whatever you individually choose to do in terms of stopping rape, you need to communicate and be accountable to your local feminists anti-rape community(ies).

But what does "accountability" really mean? How does one act it out? These are fairly specific questions that need to be answered between you and the feminist survivor advocacy organizations you are working with. In general, being accountable means, first, not doing anything that runs counter to what survivors or the feminist leadership need and want. This doesn't necessarily mean doing everything they want, but it does mean that we listen to them first in terms of how we can best work with men. What kinds of events, actions, services, or programs do they want us to develop? Accountability means being responsive to them. They may be concerned about how we are working, and about the kinds of information we share with men. It means we must be as clear about the process of doing what we do as we are about the end point of a rape-free society! It means creating a relationship built on trust and respect where they know they can come to us if they need to.

A number of difficult and challenging issues arise when thinking through accountability. What happens, for example, if the rape crisis center explicitly denies any feminist analysis or direction? (It is not our place to judge or decide which women are and aren't feminists; we go by their self-definitions). Some programs focus totally on the mental-health issues of healing from sexual assault and don't address issues of power, control, heterosexism, racism, and sexism in relation to rape and deny any feminist analysis. Or what if feminist groups are divided in their thinking about men's involvement in the movement? One program may support men working with men and want to work closely with you, while another may be skeptical and oppose the false impression you create about "some" men being "safe" for women. Accountability is fairly easy to discuss, but it often gets quite difficult to live. Again, being accountable does not necessarily mean doing what feminist leaders want us to do. It isn't easy, but as long as we keep the lines of communication explicitly open, and be clear with feminist leaders about how we are making decisions—and involving them in our decision-making processes—then the difficulties can be kept to a minimum.

## SELF CARE

It is also important to be aware of how doing this work affects us personally. This is painful, difficult, and seemingly-endless work, and it hurts to examine something as ugly as rape this closely. We need to identify and develop ways to take excellent care of ourselves in the process. I want to cover a variety of issues that arise for men doing this work. But I also want first to acknowledge that there is a lot that is very empowering and liberating about doing anti-rape work. As hard, difficult, and frustrating as it is—and as impossible as it often feels—I absolutely love doing this work. It's exciting and invigorating to be with men and watch as they struggle with these issues and come to terms with what it all means. A lot of the work is also really fun, such as organizing actions, putting together fund-raisers or concerts. I'm not making light of the issues—these are heavy, but we don't necessarily need to get weighed down to the point of inaction by them.

As described earlier during the continuum discussion, sexual violence is the ugly end of sexuality. This isn't to say that rape is sexually motivated—it is still about power and control. But it is connected, for men, to other issues of sexuality and sexual expression. As such, many people working in the movement experience some time when being sexually intimate becomes difficult. It can become very challenging to be intimate in a sexual way. Even when we *know* that we aren't doing anything abusive, manipulative, or controlling, we all still have images of sexual violence in our head. After spending an entire day looking at issues of sexual violence it can be damn near impossible to be sexual that night. Feelings of vulnerability, fear, anger, and disgust are common for people who begin addressing these issues.

Anti-rape work is difficult for the audience, and is often painful and stressful for the presenter(s). The emotional response is only human, and the pain must be acknowledged. For you who are becoming active, you need to consider ways to actively incorporate self-care in your day-to-day living, as well as when doing anti-rape organizing, activism, or educating. Think about those little incidentals like getting enough sleep, eating well, having fun, getting hugs, and having time to think about other things. What do you need in order to be your best, and do your best work? What can you set up to be completely available during the presentation for the audience? How can you ensure that you continue to be available to do anti-rape work in ten years? These are important questions for you to ask yourself, and plan for.

The self-examination in this work often results in seeing behaviors and attitudes in ourselves that uncover our connection with "those" men who are violent. It's important to stay aware that you are not alone in this struggle, and that many of us have gone through a similar process. Stay committed to getting through. Set up the process so you can get the support you need. One of the best ways to get that support is through a men stopping rape group (often called Men Against Rape [MAR] groups).

The feeling that men are bad or wrong is not true. Those feelings need to be validated, but men are not the problem. Rape, abusiveness, harassment, heterosexism, racism, and sexism are the problems. We need to distinguish between the person and the behavior, and find ways to support ourselves emotionally, spiritually, and physically at the same time that we are working to clean up our behaviors and attitudes.

# SEVEN

# MOVING ON
*Building, Sustaining, and Maintaining
Men Against Rape Groups*

UNDERLYING MUCH OF what I say is a strong desire to see
thousands of pro-feminist men's anti-rape and anti-violence groups
develop across the continent and around the planet. I want to see men
come together to discuss these issues, and to plan how to dismantle this
system of domination and control that keeps men in a position as
victimizer or threat. *That* is our work, men's work. We *are* in a position to
effectively counter the "male lobby" that continues to advocate the
maintenance of male supremacy. We *can* turn the incidence of rape
around and see a decrease! We have the ability to create a world where *all*
women, children, and men are safe from the threat of men's violence.
With local grassroots groups of men organizing in *your* communities
around the country, men's anti-rape efforts can effectively work to reduce
the incidents of men's violence, as well as educate other men in how to
end men's violence.

The reasons for developing such men's groups are many. We need to
support each other in this work, to develop opportunities for men to come
together to discuss these issues, and to create new ways for overthrowing
patriarchy. We need to come together to expose and deconstruct the
myths that keep us limited (man as "rescuer"; the John Wayne hero image;
men as unfeeling; men as detached; white men and men of color not being
able to work effectively and respectfully together; and heterosexual, bi,
and gay men divided from each other). We need to come together to
prevent burnout and isolation. We need to come together to more
effectively organize against men's violence and the anti-feminist men's
movements, to come together as a voice to counter the male supremacist

129

voices. As we do so, we exponentially increase our creativity, collective intelligence, and effectiveness against men's violence.

Furthermore, it is easier for us to be confronted on our sexism, racism, and homophobia when it comes from someone we have some connection and history with. It is easier to grow in support, and be willing to be confronted and confront each other on the inappropriate behaviors that arise, if we are part of an ongoing organization. As we develop men's groups, we need to be careful not to get caught in the habit of focusing on the support and on the "feel good"s about being men. Sitting around a living room drinking hot tea and talking about these issues is an important step, but that alone won't stop rape. Men's groups are a foundation from which we can take action.

Forming, joining, and maintaining healthy Men Against Rape (MAR) organizations in our local communities is probably one of the most powerful and effective steps any of us can take against sexual violence. This kind of large scale social change that I'm advocating here and that is required in order to end male violence does not happen overnight, nor does it happen in Washington, DC. This kind of change happens in Peoria, Waterloo, Santa Cruz, Olympia, Kerrville, Lansing, Victoria, Toronto, Tempe, and a thousand smaller cities and towns throughout this country. Change happens, as we saw with Mothers Against Drunk Driving (MADD), when people come together in their communities to demand change. To stop rape, we need to organize and focus on our towns, cities, schools, businesses, neighborhoods, and homes. Get together with men in and around *your* community to talk about this book and others like it, and to begin organizing. What about forming a group in San Antonio that focuses on raising enough money so that the rape crisis centers and battered women's shelters can serve every woman and child who calls for assistance or support? How about creating a group in Yonkers that educates from elementary school through college on the issues of sexual violence and men's responsibility? How about Fairbanks organizing a men's activist group to confront these issues on the street? And how about groups like these in every state? We cannot individually change the world, but we can change our piece of it. We cannot do it all, but we can do something!

The past few years have seen a dramatic increase in the number of men's groups in the country. The vast majority of these do nothing on issues of men's violence, but instead have gathered to discover the "warrior within." Instead, we need to gather to discuss the ways that men are acting out our "internal warrior" against women, children, and other men *all the time!* Men need, instead, to get in touch with our "internal dove" in a way that interrupts patterns of men's violence. We can also look at how these groups have organized and use that as a model for developing groups that discuss the greatest vision of "being a man"—being a man that lives, breathes, and *is* peace, equality, and justice.

Gather together with your male friends to discuss how to organize whatever makes the most sense for you in your community. Begin by putting announcements in the church bulletins, newspapers, and alternative presses serving the peace or other communities. If there is a local NOW chapter or other feminist group that includes men, ask them if they have male participants who may be interested in joining, and if they would make an announcement. Put up flyers in the restaurants, bookstores, gift shops, and copy centers. Don't expect an overwhelming response, for you will likely end up with a handful of men—perhaps three or four who are interested. Start with what you have to start with.

Begin simply—talk with each other. You need to develop some trust and willingness to be honest with each other. After some time, the group will take on a life of its own. As you talk about issues raised in this book, relate them to your personal life. What did you find out about yourself while reading the book? What have you discovered as you've discussed parts of the book with each other? How does what I say here relate to your personal sexual experiences?

Getting clear in your own head and heart about these issues is important, and having a men's discussion group or consciousness-raising group is certainly necessary. But it will do nothing to stop rape, protect victim-survivors, or confront the "rape apologists." Doing that requires that you move out of the living room and take other forms of action. A great way to begin is to organize fund-raisers for local battered women shelters or rape crisis centers. Contact local programs and see what their financial needs are. They may be fine financially (it's doubtful, but you never know), but have other needs that you can fill. Organizing a fund-raiser is rather easy and can be as simple as organizing a "house party." Ask the center if you can use their mailing list to send out invitations, as well as invite your friends, co-workers, neighbors, and fellow students, and there you go—you've just organized a fund-raiser. You can go to bars, clubs, restaurants, or theaters and see if they are willing to donate a portion of a night's proceeds in exchange for your working the door. The ideas for fund-raising are limitless. Be creative, have fun with it, and make time to evaluate how it went afterwards.

One benefit of staging fund-raisers is that it develops skills in organizing such as writing, talking, meeting people, bringing people together, and motivating people towards action. Those skills are then transferable to other kinds of activities such as organizing educational opportunities in schools or businesses, demonstrating against rape, holding a men's conference, bringing in speakers, or writing a book. As you develop your skills in reaching out and motivating, you'll find that your self-confidence also increases—which then becomes an upwardly spiraling cycle.

Organizing a fund-raiser for a local program also begins the long process of establishing a relationship of accountability and trust with a feminist group. The best way to build a relationship is to trust each other. They need to know that they can talk with you and that you will be responsive. Find out from your local program(s) what you can do on a more ongoing basis that is most beneficial to them. Let them set the agenda for the work you do—particularly at the beginning.

## STAYING ACCOUNTABLE TO FEMINISTS

The subject of accontability has been covered, but it can't be discussed too much. In this section, I will focus on the specifics of men and men's groups being accountable to feminists and feminist groups.

Our culture continues to misunderstand what accountability means. For most people, accountability connotes the eerie sense of having some police state watching over our shoulders waiting for us to make a mistake and jump down our throats. For my purposes here, however, accountability is better described as being responsive to the feminist leadership. I define this as listening to their concerns, being responsible for our actions, communicating on an ongoing basis, and being willing to acknowledge when we make mistakes. Being accountable means being willing to take an accounting of our behaviors and take response-ability for our choices. It means being responsive to the women in our life and the women we are working with, as well as to the women and women's groups that are working most directly with survivors of men's violence.

When developing pro-feminist men's groups, it is absolutely essential that we develop strong lines of communication with the local feminist leadership—the first step in developing a relationship. It is vital that local feminists and feminist organizations are aware of what we are doing. At times allies act without first checking in with the people who are most directly affected and so end up hurting the people they were hoping to act in support of, despite the best of intentions. For example, a couple of years ago, I assisted in organizing a fund-raiser for a local rape crisis program without making sure that we had been in touch with them about the fund-raiser. As a result we organized the fund-raiser on the same evening as they had organized a honors dinner—which was also a fund-raiser—and supporters of the center were forced to choose which way they wanted to support the organization. We lessen the likelihood of this kind of mistake by maintaining open lines of communication with the local organizations and maintaining an awareness of their activities.

Second, it is common sense and common courtesy that we communicate with our sisters when we are involved with organizing or activism that involves their lives. Men's violence is deadly—according to some estimates, as many as fifteen women a day in the U.S. are killed by men's violence. Feminism, and feminist organizing against men's violence, has been the primary voice against men's violence, and has offered support to the victim-survivors. We need to remember that we are dealing with women's lives.

For men, living an anti-rape lifestyle is a choice. For most women, there is no choice—this is about being alive! Because we choose to do anti-violence work, we can choose to stop doing the work, and choose to be violent at any time. Most of you are thinking, "I could never choose to hurt anybody." And maybe in your particular case that is true. But it's doubtful that you can't conceive of ever considering hurting somebody, and that you haven't already. Additionally, the women we are working with don't know of your commitment to nonviolence! Men of every category and class have raped: "nice" men, sensitive men, pro-feminist men, activist men, peacekeeping men, nonviolent men, students, athletic men, professors, politicians, and fraternity brothers. In order to be safe, women *must* maintain some level of awareness. They *know* that anti-rape work is a choice for men, and a choice they can choose to stop.

Women also know, painfully, that any man, no matter what he may say, may choose to harass, abuse, rape, or act out other oppressive behaviors. A prime example is the 1992 case of Senator Bob Packwood (Democrat from Oregon), who has been one of the strongest supporters of women and women's issues in Congress. During the election campaign, he was accused of sexually harassing behaviors, which he summarily dismissed. Several weeks after the election, he finally admitted that he had harassed these women and apologized. I don't want to condemn Senator Packwood; that would be hypocritical (although I do condemn his harassing behaviors). The point is that any and all of us may be guilty of the same kinds of behaviors, the same kind of discrepancy between our personal actions and our public statements. And there is no way for women to know that simply based on our words.

At times being accountable is certainly difficult to manage. Feminism is by no means a single entity. It is a complex multitude of varying beliefs, interpretations, and ideas about what equality and liberation mean. As such, being accountable to feminism can be confusing. As John Stoltenberg has asked, "To which feminists are we accountable?"

For example, on Father's Day in 1988, I organized a demonstration for nonviolent fathers in response to a demonstration organized in support of Eric Foretich. Eric Foretich was the ex-husband of Dr. Elizabeth Morgan, who, at that time, had spent nearly two years in the Washington, DC, jail for contempt of court. She and Dr. Foretich were in a custody battle over their child Hilary, who alleged that Dr. Foretich had sexually abused her. In order to keep her child safe, Dr. Morgan placed Hilary into hiding, and was jailed for contempt of court. On Father's Day, 1988, Dr. Foretich and his supporters held a demonstration in his support at the department of justice in Washington DC.

I organized a counterdemonstration for nonviolent fathers at the same site. I tried to show that rather than spending time defending himself and denying the allegations (which I believe to be true), a more appropriate role for a nonviolent father would be to try and determine who the hell had abused his child (there were never any doubts that Hilary had been abused). Two days before the event, we were contacted by Dr. Morgan's support committee, with whom we had been in frequent contact throughout the organizing. They shared with us Dr. Morgan's discomfort with our plan to go through with the action in her name. At the same time, a fair number of feminist activists strongly supported the demonstration. I was left in a position of determining to which feminists I was going to be accountable, and of trying to balance that with the desperate need I felt to make this statement. I didn't know how I could not follow through with the demonstration, despite the concerns of Dr. Morgan—but she was the woman whose life was directly affected: she was in jail, and it was her child was in danger.

After a very long night of ongoing deliberations, we decided that we would go through with the demonstration, but that we would remove Dr. Morgan's name from all of the information and publicity. As best we could, we took the focus off of the specific case and onto the dynamics of fathers who don't act in a responsible way with their children, especially after divorce. This is but a small example of the kinds of dilemmas that can arise when attempting to stay accountable and organize from a pro-feminist perspective.

# KEEP ON KEEPING ON:
## MAINTAINING THE HEALTH
## OF YOUR MEN'S GROUP

Sustaining a healthy men's anti-rape group requires constant reevaluating, restructuring, flexibility, and a willingness to grow and develop in ways that you may or may not be prepared for. It also requires a mix of ingredients: individual and group support, direct action, fundraising, challenging group members towards growth, time for play, and time for rest. This intricate balance is often hard to come by and may be quite elusive, but is necessary in order to sustain a healthy men's anti-rape organization. It is much easier to build these into the beginning, rather than to try and bring these aspects into the process after the group has already begun to develop.

Have at least one person be responsible for the needs of the group as a whole and its members as well as for planning future growth and development (i.e., a coordinator or coordinating committee). It is certainly easier and healthier if these responsibilities can be shared; however, this is seldom the case. Every member of the group has part of the responsibility to think about the other members, and about the group as a whole, but usually one person does the active work around keeping the group going and healthy. Coordinating work includes thinking about arranging meeting places and times, special needs of group members, agenda proposals, the personal lives and difficult times of various members of the group (always a popular subject), money and the financial needs of the group, the general feel of the group and how the group is doing, and ensuring that everyone has the opportunity to have input—including those who aren't present at the meetings.

Coordinating doesn't necessarily mean making the decisions and doing the work, but rather making sure that the decisions get made and that those decisions are communicated to all members and that the work gets done. Thinking about special needs includes being aware of and sensitive to allergies, accessibility, transportation, and child care needs of the members. I prefer to set the agenda at the beginning of each meeting, but it is also helpful to already have some ideas from which to "springboard." Think about the process of the meetings and the group as a whole: Do folks need to take a break and spend some time just having fun together without working on issues? Are there some unstated or underlying difficulties that aren't being processed with the group?

It isn't necessary for one person to take on all or any of these tasks all of the time. To build some shared sense of ownership of the organization, and to develop leadership skills in as many of the members as possible, it is best if these roles are shared between several members. This can be difficult, but we certainly have the innate creativity to come up with ways to meet these needs.

Maintain some kind of history of the group, preferably written. Describe, and have other members describe, when, where, how it got started. Who was involved in the early development? What kinds of activities has the group been involved in? What about the parties or fun times? and so on. Acknowledging these steps is important, and celebrating our steps is vital, no matter how small they may seem. Keeping that history present also encourages the continual flow of the group's energy. As new folks come in, and folks who have been involved move on, it helps to have some sense of roots so that people feel connected. Having a written history certainly makes this task much easier.

Whether you are linked by geography or by interest, it is good to be connected with other groups. People need to feel connected to something bigger, so build on these connections. Good examples of where to go to develop these connections include your local rape crisis center, battered women's shelter, or women's center; men's groups in other towns or states; the Men's Anti-Rape Resource Center [MARC]; Ending Men's Violence Network; the National Coalition Against Sexual Assault (NCASA); the National Coalition Against Domestic Violence (NCADV), and peace groups or other progressive groups in your area. (See the list of contacts at the back of this book.)

## TAKING ACTION

When choosing actions, balance the need for attention on the issues with the resources at your disposal. It can be tempting to try to organize big actions. However, in small groups the work will get divided among fewer and fewer participants as people burn out. With that in mind, it is important to think about what needs are specific to your area, what your group's needs are, what resources you have, and what your expectations are for the activity. After doing an event, schedule some time to evaluate what you did and how you did it. Also, allow time for everyone to process the experience. Then go play, take some time off, and do what you need to do to reenergize and recreate.

Funding is one concern that continues to plague men's anti-violence groups. Most of our actions require some money (e.g., publicity, printing, postage, and permits). As a result, we need to spend some of our energy on the building of financial resources. Should we be raising money for these programs when there aren't adequate services for all the victim/survivors who need them? I do not mean to say that the programs are inadequate, but that most rape crisis and battered women's programs do not have adequate funding to offer the services needed for everyone who calls. Nearly every program has to turn some survivors away. Therefore, when we do fund-raising for our programs, we need to ask if we are taking money away from the survivor service organizations and thus the survivors themselves. In answering this question, we need to realize that, by and large, we are looking to the same pools of money for funding. One way to answer those concerns is to have dual fund-raisers for ourselves and a local agency (rape crisis center, battered woman's shelter, woman's center, or other organization). Be creative.

The kinds of action that men can organize are limitless. We can organize child care for feminist events such as the Take Back the Night marches. Or we can organize a men's discussion while the women march. By creating an opportunity for the men who attend Take Back the Night (TBTN) events to get something concrete, we increase the likelihood that men can do something a month after the TBTN. Additionally, the point of TBTN is for *women* to reclaim the night. Women don't need men! If the point is for men to show solidarity with women, we can organize many other ways to do that.

Numerous other ideas are also woth a try. Organize a speak-out for men against violence, do a read-in at a local bookstore, do a candlelight vigil on an evening that may hold special significance in your community, or organize a Give Back the Night event that demonstrates men taking proactive steps for women to be safer. In 1989, DC Men Against Rape in Washington, DC, constructed a women's memorial wall. On it, they listed 51,000 women's names (using pseudonyms) to represent the 51,000 women killed by men in the U.S. during a seventeen-year period—the same period of time that the U.S. was waging war against Vietnam. They then placed this wall across from the Vietnam Memorial and used this visual to speak out against all war. They also drew connections: It was due to public outcry that the U.S. ended the war against Vietnam, and it will be because of men's public outcry that men end the war against women.

In 1991, BrotherPeace in St. Paul, Minnesota, draped a series of banners denouncing men's violence during rush hour from the overpasses along the interstates surrounding the city. There's no telling how many people they got to with their message, but it's safe to assume thousands. In 1992, during the Men and Masculinity Conference, a collective of men from a variety of local men's groups organized a speak-out against pornography at the headquarters of Playboy in Chicago. The ideas are limited only by your creativity and your resources.

One important date to keep in mind is the third Saturday in October. This is BrotherPeace Day, the international day of men taking action to end men's violence. On this day, local groups organize local actions to correspond with others that are going on elsewhere in the world. The focus is on men taking direct action. BrotherPeace is organized by the Ending Men's Violence Network (address listed in the contacts list) and over the years conferences, demonstrations, concerts, marches, and hundreds of other events have occurred.

## BURNOUT

We need to be aware of a number of factors about burnout and its prevention. When we first get started in this work, we tend to want to "do everything now!!!" This can be a very damaging pattern, one that should be examined closely. Pressuring ourselves for immediate results really encourages burnout as well as reinforces traditional male patterns of intervening and helping. I'm not advocating hopelessness, for there are great reasons for hope; however, I also don't want to encourage "pie in the sky" thinking. Male violence will not end tomorrow, no matter how much we give or how hard we try today. We're in this for the long haul. As such, you need to plan to be involved for the long haul.

To interrupt our patterns of violence and oppression we need to counter our patterns of male supremacy—and this includes traditionally male patterns of helping. That male tradition of identifying a problem, coming to the rescue, and "fixing it" before we take off to solve the next problem is not conducive to creating long-term solutions to difficult and complex problems. Additionally, men are taught to "give it our all." This pattern has manifested itself in workaholism and working till we drop. Not only is this not good for ourselves, it reinforces our isolation and is detrimental to the movement.

Take some time to acknowledge the work that is being done, and the fact that we are making progress. While these steps are very small when compared to where we need to be, when we take a step back and notice that we have made some progress, there is reason to celebrate LOUDLY.

Just coming together, thinking about these issues, and putting out our energy into the universe makes a difference and should be recognized as worthwhile. Take some time to examine the need to make a difference. Part of that is very human, and part of that is very male in a controlling and supremacist way.

A host of other very personal issues arise when we start organizing as men around ending men's violence. Some men get involved because it seems like the politically correct thing to do. However, we need to continuously examine how we encourage rape behavior on a daily basis. This process can become very painful, difficult, and frustrating, particularly when we can go across the street and work to end the arms race without as much self-reflection.

Men are generally isolated from one other. When we take a stand on these kinds of issues, we seem to isolate ourselves even further from other men. This can be very painful and unhealthy—and can lead to burnout.

Finally, when doing anti-rape work, you will get in touch with women and men who have been victimized, and you will hear their stories *a lot*. Rarely do I offer a presentation in a mixed-gender audience where women in the audience don't disclose their victimization experiences. It becomes really hard to keep hearing these stories day after day, since they stay in your head and follow you home. You may find yourself going to movies, seeing scenes that are disturbing but not necessarily evil, and your reaction (which is magnified because of the stories that are still running through your head) is one of indescribable anguish and anger. Getting into this issue too heavily can wear people down and result in burnout. The feelings are intense. Make space and opportunity for you to process the feelings that arise and maintain some balance.

## PREVENTING BURNOUT

Hugs are one of my personal favorite ways of avoiding burnout. It's important to receive nurturing. Maintain an awareness of people's expectations for themselves, each other, and the group. Examine with each other where these expectations may be coming from. Ask yourselves: What happens to the disappointment and frustration that may come up? How can we readjust the expectations so that they don't lead to frustration? Frustration and disappointment tend to come from unmet expectations. You can either choose to not get frustrated by unmet expectations, to reevaluate your expectations so that you aren't frustrated, or to express your frustration and disappointment.

Set up activities to counter the isolation. The first step is to acknowledge it as early as you can. Build in ways to contradict these feelings with friends and in group. Create a situation so that you aren't alone. If you are, it lessens your effectiveness. When people voice feelings of isolation, encourage some fun time together. Find out what makes it difficult to share and connect with others, especially with other men. Often, much of the difficulty in connecting with other men is related to male guilt. Spend some time supporting each other.

Build in time to reevaluate and reassess where we are and where we are going. Make this time happen not only after an event but throughout a group's or person's development. Sit back and evaluate where you are, examine the direction from which you have come, and look at where you are heading. Make the process you and the gorup is going through conscious and strategic.

I also cannot stress enough how vital and radical it is for us to take good care of ourselves. We must make sure we get enough sleep and exercise, eat, meet our spiritual needs, and can take a break from these issues. All of these need to happen not in their own right but also to contradict the message that many community activists buy into that "involvement means being overextended." Check in with each other and be creative with how you are supportive of each other; meetings *can* be scheduled at dances or movies. Men's anti-rape groups are valuable additions to the anti-violence movement. We must provide programs that will build toward the world that we all envision. One step towards that end is to remain healthy both individually and collectively, creating a radical contradiction to the lie we are all taught about how men are "supposed" to be isolated even when together.

# EIGHT

# RESPONDING
# TO SURVIVORS

FOR THE PURPOSES of this discussion, I will assume that the person disclosing their rape experience to you is an adult. I will be referring to both female and male survivors. While many of the skills I will discuss will also relate to child and adolescent survivors, the differences warrant separating the discussion. What follows is a brief description of how to listen in a supportive way. If you are interested in a more thorough discussion, a number of excellent books are listed in the bibliography, and I would suggest contacting your local rape crisis center.

Inevitably there are people in your life, women and men, who have survived sexual victimization(s). Some will have been raped as children (euphemistically known as "incest" or "molestation"), others will have been raped as adolescents, and still others as adults. Some will have been attacked by people they know very well, like parents, siblings, or boyfriends; others by people they hardly knew, such as classmates or first dates; and still others by strangers. We need to know these listening skills not only for the survivors in our lives but also for ourselves. In my experience, and in that of many other men, once it becomes evident that we are "safe" people for survivors to tell their stories to, they do.

Many of us find ourselves in a position of offering support to friends who have been victimized. Be mindful of the ways you offer support, since it can be a power trip. Men are taught to ride in on white horses and carry people away from trouble. We're supposed to slay the dragon and rescue the woman from danger. As I will explain, rescuing does little good for anybody and we need to ensure that we aren't in a position of one up*man*ship in relation to the person we are supporting—which is exactly where the "hero" or "helper" role puts us.

As Robin Morgan explained in *Demon Lover*, the hero doing the rescuing requires the villain. The separation between the lover, hero, rescuer, and the villain is minimal, and often they are two sides of the same coin, since both the hero and the villian keep the victim in a powerless, hopeless, and helpless position. This position is of no value to women, or to survivors, and it only maintains male domination. Women are not powerless or helpless, but rather are strong, powerful, and completely able to protect and take care of themselves! Survivors don't need men. They can and do meet their own needs and find ways to heal from being victimized on their own. They've proven their strength, power, and resourcefulness by surviving the attack(s).

Being a man and supportive requires that we mint an entirely new coin. It is important to care and offer support, but *thoughtful and caring* support. Rather than "helping" or "rescuing" (read: taking over), let us offer support in ways the survivor we are talking with describes as appropriate and supportive. Let us recognize and celebrate their incredible strength and power, while at the same time being aware that they have been deeply hurt. Survivors are not "poor" victims (that's why we use the word survivor). They aren't "damaged"—just hurt. So be there, be supportive, and listen.

Listening to male survivors can raise particular issues. Men tend not to have the same access to our feelings as women do, and rarely have the language to describe those feelings. So being supportive of male survivors can be much more difficult. They may not have the language to describe what happened, how they feel, nor what they need (asking for help is especially difficult for men). Men often feel as if their manhood has been damaged as a result of being sexually victimized, and admitting that they've been abused can stir up those feelings. We misunderstand when we think that men who rape men are gay; most men who rape men are heterosexual—the rape is not motivated by sexual desire. But it drives us to feel that the survivor must have been in some way effeminate. Further, a "real man" would have protected himself and fought to the death before being raped. Finally, "real men" don't ask for help. These patterns all become tied together and can create a lot of confusion for the one trying to be supportive.

One final note: Healing from sexual violence is an inherently political act. As feminists have demonstrated repeatedly, and I noted in the first chapter, rape is a political act. By definition, therefore, healing is political. In our society rape "victims" are just that—"victims." They are supposed to stay silent about what they went through, stay hidden, and stay powerless. When survivors refuse to stay in that position, and speak out, act up, and reclaim their rightful place—out in the open with the full sun shining on them—they stand right in the face of patriarchy. Healing is political, and assisting someone in their healing is political.

## CRISIS INTERVENTION

When friends disclose their history to you, the first and most crucial point to ascertain is *are they currently safe?* (physically, emotionally, and spiritually). Obviously, this depends upon the specific circumstances of the disclosure, and what they are disclosing. For example, are they calling you from a pay phone immediately after an attack, or telling you of an attack that occurred many years ago? Be careful because there may be a definitional difference between how you and the survivor defines safety. Ask them if they feel safe and examine what needs to happen to increase the feelings of safety. They may not know if they feel safe, or know how to get to a feeling of relative safety—remember, this is a person who has been attacked in a terribly intimate manner. You need to stay aware of what is happening during the disclosure. When people are in a panic or a crisis, they may not be thinking clearly, so you need to be aware of these issues. Telling someone about past sexual victimization is almost always stressful, and may itself create a near-crisis situation for the person.

If the attack is recent, it makes sense to encourage going to the hospital and calling the local rape crisis center. Survivors can go into emotional shock and may not feel internal injuries. Pregnancy tests can be administered for female survivors and the "morning after" pill can be prescribed if desired. The hospital can also gather and record physical evidence like blood, semen, hair, skin, and bruises that would be invaluable evidence if the survivor should choose to follow through with criminal prosecution (a choice they don't have to make immediately). The rape crisis center can also offer emotional support, explain what is happening procedurally, inform them (and you) of their rights, and advocate for them.

Survivors can choose at any point whether to file a report with the police. Because rape or attempted rape is a felony, it will be the state that is bringing charges; the survivor is a witness. Therefore, it isn't "their" case. They can also file what is called a "Jane or John Doe" report, which is an anonymous report that gives the information about the attack and the perpetrator(s). This is kept on file with the police in the case the perpetrator strikes again, and can help build a future case. Survivors don't have to choose immediately, although it is easier if they choose to contact the police immediately so that the evidence will be gathered appropriately. For more information about police procedures, and suggestions for legal and hospital intervention, contact your local rape crisis center. Each jurisdiction has somewhat different rules and policies and the local rape crisis center is the expert.

Throughout the disclosing process continue to reinforce that whatever they did in order to survive was *exactly the correct thing to do*. Had they done anything differently, they might have been killed. For many survivors, this fear of death is one of the greatest fears, regardless of whether the rapist made any overt threats. Acknowledging that they survived an attack not only validates their fears but also reinforces their strength and personal power and interrupts the self-blaming that is likely to occur. Regardless of how long ago the attack may have happened, many of the initial feelings can be stirred up during disclosure. Keep reminding this person that they have, in fact, survived!

Aside from reminding survivors of their strength and courage, it is vital to reinforce that *they did nothing to deserve the attack!* As basic as that may sound, most survivors experience a great deal of self-blame. This emotion is frequently masked by questions of "Why?" such as "Why did he do it?" "Why didn't I leave sooner?" "Why didn't I scream?" and "Why couldn't I tell?" It is safe to assume the self-blame is present and to respond to "why" questions as if they are self-blame. The value and necessity of contradicting those internal (and often external) messages cannot be overemphasized!

## STEP-BY-STEP LISTENING

Throughout the process, it is important for you to try to divorce yourself from doing the survivor's healing work for them. *They* need to go through *their* healing at *their* pace, and that cannot be determined or forced by any other person. In trying to support survivors through their healing, many men make the mistake of pushing the survivor or of trying to do the healing for them. Remember that one of the main goals of the healing process is empowerment, and that survivors need to recognize the power and strength they have. Taking over doesn't reinforce their personal strength and empowerment can't be given, but must develop from within.

Disclosing sexual victimizing experiences is an extremely courageous act. Recognize the courage and strength it took for them to share their experiences with you. You need not know any more details than they are willing and comfortable offering. If you do find yourself "needing" details, recognize that this is your need, not theirs, and it is not appropriate for you to ask for them. Your role is to meet your friend's needs and to let them set the pace of their disclosure.

Throughout the listening and healing process, maintain an awareness of your own feelings about the attack(s) as well as about the survivor. It is not the responsibility of the survivor to meet your needs, but that doesn't mean that you aren't going to have needs and that you don't have the right to have them met. When you begin feeling overwhelmed, or think that their needs may be beyond your capabilities, acknowledge that. When done thoughtfully and caringly, to suggest they may benefit from seeing someone who is trained to work with survivors isn't rejection, it's supportive honesty.

Be patient and gentle. Healing from sexual assault is a lifelong process, because the person was attacked to their very core. People healing from sexual assault will have times when they aren't bothered by the experience. Yet, those same feelings can be stirred to the surface by anniversaries, "subtle" reminders, or other triggers that remind them of the attack. A survivor needs space to heal on their terms, and at their pace. You can best be supportive by encouraging them to take all the time they need, and reminding them that they survived the attack, and they will survive the memories. Let them tell you how you can best be supportive, and talk with others about how they can best be supportive.

Most important, *listen* when responding to survivors. Listen to what *they* need, want, and expect. This interaction becomes tricky, particularly when you are emotionally attached. It is difficult, at times, to separate yourself from your needs, wants, and expectations long enough to listen to the survivor; however, in this situation, their needs come first.

Being a man and responding to survivors poses certain particular difficulties. We are socialized to believe that we are supposed to "take care of" difficulties by "fixing" them. According to male socialization patterns, men are supposed to go in, repair whatever is broken, and leave—neat, concise, and simple. As Deborah Tannen points out in *You Just Don't Understand: Men and Women in Conversation*, men tend to listen to problems as part of a process of trying to find the solution. Unfortunately, we cannot "fix" rape. Men cannot, and should not, "fix" what happened to someone who has been raped. Generally, there aren't any clear actions to take. Many men immediately want to "get the guy," and "put the hurt on." However, when responding to survivors' needs you must continuously ask yourself, "How is this behavior going to assist them in their healing?" Quite frankly, attacking the man who raped your sister, mother, son, woman-friend, or housemate will not help them heal. Listening carefully to a sexually victimized friend often requires that men learn a host of new skills.

Many emotions arise in a man when someone close to him is raped: anger, guilt, relief that they survived, sadness, frustration, and confusion are common. Because men are not generally taught adequate skills for defining and processing these feelings, they are often expressed in unhealthy, sometimes self-destructive ways. This emotional baggage can prevent our being truly present for the survivor. Men need to learn to identify these feelings and express them openly and honestly. However, remember that it is not the survivor's responsibility to respond to our responses to their being attacked; we can go elsewhere (like a MAR group) to get this support.

People in pain and in the process of healing often just need to share this process and their pain. The best thing we can do is to listen well. It isn't easy to listen to someone you care about share their pain. But it is necessary in this situation to begin challenging our typical patterns. Learning to listen is one of the most valuable skills men can learn.

Being in a supportive role is terribly difficult, but can also be incredibly rewarding. Allow the survivor to define the rules of the relationship—how they are most comfortable being with you, what kind of relationship they want, and how they want to express the relationship. Be clear about what are you and are not willing to do, and be careful and thoughtful about what you are agreeing to do, particularly with survivors of childhood sexual trauma. At the same time, be careful and thoughtful for yourself: Remember that you need and deserve as much warm and caring attention as does your friend. Although you will never know what the healing process is like for them, you also have needs and the right to have your needs met.

## RAPE TRAUMA SYNDROME*

Rape Trauma Syndrome (RTS) describes the process survivors often go through when healing from sexual violence. It should be taken as a loose guide, since survivors' individual healing process is determined by many variables. There is no way to predetermine how someone may respond. However, *as a guide*, RTS has proven very beneficial in assisting people who support survivors through healing.

*This is taken from the work of Ann Wolbert Burgess and Lynda Little Holmstrom in *Rape: Victims of Crisis*, 1974.

## Immediate Reaction

Immediately after an attack, or after disclosure, survivors often experience and exhibit a wide range of emotional responses. You can best respond to this attack, and to your friend, as a crisis. Think actively about this person and what their needs are. Consider what's happening around you and them, and think about how you can best be there for them. But also remember that there are two parts to every crisis (as the Chinese so well know, the Chinese character for crisis represents both parts): danger and opportunity.

Generally, this phase is relatively short-term, but it may last as long as several weeks, and may recur throughout the healing process. Survivors often experience emotional shock and disbelief as well as intense feelings of self-blame not only for the attack, but also for any negative consequences that may result from their disclosing. During this stage of the healing, there are typically two main sets of emotions displayed: "expressed" and "controlled."

The expressed emotional responses include anger, which may be internalized and is frequently attached to self-blame (this is often intensified for female survivors); fear or anxiety of being alone, of being at home, and of going out; grief and profound levels of sadness, particularly if the perpetrator is a friend or loved one; and shame which is couched as feeling dirty or an inability to get clean.

The controlled emotional responses are harder to readily identify. These emotions may be masked while the survivor appears calm and composed. For example, acting as if she or he is "fine" with the abuse, but keeping themself busy so as to not really feel anything.

Often there are physical reactions to the abuse as well. Like the emotional responses, these too will frequently reappear whenever survivors disclose past abuse, although to varying degrees of intensity. Some of the physical reactions include disturbances of sleep or eating patterns, a difficulty with physical touch, and the sensation of physical pain (which may or may not be directly associated with the area attacked), and panic attacks.

## Long-Term Process

Often referred to as the "reorganization" phase of healing, survivors use the long-term period to reorganize their lives after the attack. It is a lengthy, gradual process in which survivors work to recover from the trauma so they can best live their life despite having been victimized. It must be emphasized that, regardless how long a survivor may take, in this phase they are not sick or handicapped. They are proceeding through their process as best they can.

There may be nightmares and continued sleep disturbances during this period, but they are likely to begin lessening in frequency and intensity. They are likely to make changes in their lifestyle as a means of reclaiming their power and sense of self.

Sexual functioning is likely be affected. Exactly how is determined by the survivor: They may desire more sexual interaction, which is more frequent with male survivors, or little or none. They themselves need to determine what kind and how much sexual interaction they have.

Suicide may be considered an option, and signs of suicidal thinking should be looked for at any time during the healing process, and particularly as they become frustrated with the difficulty they encounter in "putting it behind them." One of the greatest tragedies of an attack is that it will always be with them, but remind them of the movement they have made. Remind them that they survived the attack, and so they can survive the experience. And they aren't stagnating—even though that is probably how it feels for them. They are moving. They may be experiencing the same feelings they've had in the past, but they are in a different place now than they were the last time they experienced those feelings. Being as concrete as you can, show them the ways they are not in the same place. Or better still, have them show you.

## DEALING WITH YOURSELF

Listening to a friend, lover, colleague, or family member describe how they've been sexually victimized is incredibly painful. You care about someone, and they are describing one of the most horrendous experiences anyone could describe—perhaps in excruciating detail. Additionally, as you become known among your friends and colleagues as someone that survivors can talk with and be supported, more and more people will come out to you. Many men and women for whom this is true describe the ways that it begins to wear them down. You may lose energy or become easily distracted when people describe their experiences to you, yet you want to be supportive. You become afraid to mention that doing anti-rape work is a part of your life (some of us even find ourselves lying from time to time about it) so that you lessen the likelihood of people coming out to you. It's very painful. As one friend described it, "I'd more easily list the names of friends who haven't come out than list the names of friends who have." You may start to assume that all your friends are survivors—the only difference being that some have come out to you, and others haven't.

All of these experiences and their cumulative impact on your life begin to wear on you. You *must* find ways to release the tension and get the stories out of your head. You and you alone know what way of receiving support works best for you. But you need to find it. It's important for you to be able to listen to the people in your life and support them. To be able to keep doing so you need to find some ways to share what you've heard. For me, one of the best places to do that is in the local Men Against Rape group. There, I can talk with men who share my experiences and who can be supportive from that shared background. It also ensures the anonymity of the person who came out to me (sometimes they don't want their stories shared beyond you—and always, *they* choose who their story is shared with and how their story is shared).

When unloading, stay focused on your experience. Retelling their story won't help you that much, because their experience isn't yours. Moreover, retelling their experience threatens their right to confidentiality. Describe what it's like for you to hear these stories, and the responses you find yourself having. Discuss the anger that bubbles to the surface (or explodes) after hearing yet another friend talk about the pain and anger of their victimization experiences. Talk about how it's affecting your life.

Another way to respond to the process of being told stories is to write down your responses. Writing is a wonderful and underutilized process for venting our feelings. You can use writing to say all that you want to say, in whatever way you may want to say it to the person(s) who hurt your friend, as well as to your friend. By writing, you don't have to worry about being "politically correct" or being supportive or how whatever you say may sound—you can just let go! You can always choose later on what to do with what you've written: share it with your friend, share it with a support network, send it in letter form to the person(s) who hurt your friend, publish it, or destroy it. But save that decision till after you've finished writing.

Along with sharing your feelings and writing them down, another useful technique is to literally get away from it. Go for a drive or a walk, go to the park or a movie, or read some trashy novel. Nobody has an emotional well deep enough to draw from endlessly in order to be supportive. Everyone must take some time to replenish their selves. Make time, and give yourself permission to do that too.

And if it's too much for you to handle, ask for help. It's okay for you to use some of the professional services as well. Call the rape crisis center or hotline and explain that you're having a hard time because you're trying to be supportive of a friend. Explain to them the impact it is having on you.

You have a right to get support as well—and to acknowledge that hearing these damn stories all the time hurts. Do it!

# NINE

# THE YEAR 2000
# AND BEYOND

W HAT WILL THE world be like when we are finally successful in our efforts to eliminate men's violence? What will it be like when women and men, children and adults, white people and people of color, heterosexuals, homosexuals, and bisexuals will be able to work, play, live, love, and laugh together in a caring, loving, and mutually respectful way? What will it be like for women to walk down the street free of fear, and for men to walk down a street free from being feared?

Imagine, those of you who are male, walking into a playground full of children and not having the children fear you, and their parents wary of you. Imagine, you who are white men, walking into a community of color and not being seen as a threat for being a member of an oppressor class. Imagine, if you will, being able to walk down any street you care to, holding hands with your same-sex friend and not fear being attacked because of heterosexism. Consider what it will be like when we will be able to have children, and the men are able to stay home without having to worry about financial survival.

All of this is truly possible. Radical feminism has offered a glimpse of such a world. All of us, all of everything takes up space in the universe. The clouds, the rocks, the plants, time, objects, animals, people; all of everything takes up space and is interconnected. What has been known for centuries by certain cultures, and what physicists are beginning to realize, is that just as it is true that we all take up space in the universe, so it is true that we have a direct and profound impact on the ways that the universe continues to function. That is true for all entities. What makes humans unique is that we are apparently the only entity that can *choose* what our impact on the universe will be.

We can choose to live our lives in keeping with the grandest vision we create. So begin thinking about it. Find someplace to be quiet and still. Relax your body, and uncross your feet and your arms. Breathe consciously and in a relaxed way—deeply and rhythmically. Close your eyes and create a picture in your mind of what a rape-free world would look like—with the most expansive definition of "rape-free" that you can come up with. Think about a world where women are not afraid to go out at night, where your housemate or friend or lover can dash out to the corner store at 3 A.M. to get some milk without being afraid. Imagine a world where no child is at risk for any kind of violence, and where gay people are free to express their partnership in any way and in any place—just like heterosexual couples.

Picture in your mind a place where men aren't feared, where you can leave a movie theater at midnight, walk back to your car and not see women afraid of you. Imagine never again having to hear a friend of yours tell you that they were victimized as a child, a young adult, or earlier that year. Imagine being at work and having a deeply felt and intense argument with a woman of a different race—a deep-down, in-your-face kind of argument that isn't muddled by racial or gender politics. Develop this picture of a world free of men's violence as fully and completely in your mind as you are able and hold onto it. (The only way we'll ever get there is to begin envisioning it.)

Now, *feel* that world—feel it in your heart, and feel it in your soul. Feel what it would be like to live in that kind of world. Notice the feelings that are coming up for you—not the feelings that arise as a result of us not being there yet, but the feelings that come up as a result of experiencing such a world. A world where we don't need to prove ourselves and our masculinity. A world where we aren't expected to be the "protector" all the time and a world where we are able to be in touch with children and in touch with the child inside of us; that playful, fun-loving, spirited, curious being that exists in each of us, but which we lose touch with in the process of "becoming men." Imagine living in a world where men and women have true friendships all the time, and one in which no woman ever again looks at you with some level of dread. Feel this world as deep in yourself as you can feel.

To make it just a bit more difficult, imagine that world being this world—tomorrow! Imagine walking down your street tomorrow evening as you come home from work, or school; living in your neighborhood; driving in your town that is now rape-free. Think about it—*feel* about it.

My vision involves all that I've described. I envision myself working at home so that I can care for my children and be an active part of their growing up. I see my partner as an active part of my life, and the children's; I see an active reciprocal participation in each other's lives—we clean together, we play together, we travel, we do different things together, we spend time away from each other. My vision is a world without gender roles—where people are allowed and encouraged to live their life however they see fit, and we see no need to add the caveat, "so long as it brings no harm to another person." I see a place where I'm able to hold my child who skins his or her knee and cry with him or her rather than telling him or her (as I was told) to "be a big boy" or "girl." I see a place where lovemaking is a positive experience for *everyone*, and sex isn't something feared or despised but celebrated and encouraged in healthful and fun ways. I see people being encouraged to experience their full creativity and to live their lives as completely as possible—with respect, dignity, and integrity.

I see a world where men are free. Where men are involved in day care and men organize the bake sales for the day care center. A world where not only do men and women work together, but where men and men work together—sharing hugs, massages, and child care. A world where we look to Congress and see a body that is truly representational, one that puts the needs of children and people first. A world where value is placed on how good we have become at supporting ourselves and each other, as communities and as a nation. We will also strive to support our neighbors all over the globe—not for our own betterment, but because we're good neighbors.

We can, you know. We deserve this kind of world. Creating a rape-free world is the best of what we can offer—and in the process we can create a new image of what "being a man" means. We have the ability to respond proactively and effectively to the issues of rape and men's violence. We can create this kind of world—a world free of rape! It's up to you, it's up to us. It's time we began!

# EXERCISES
# AND
# TEACHING
# OUTLINES

> It should not be up to men to give women what is rightfully theirs.
> —Frederick Douglass

WHAT FOLLOWS IS a number of exercises and outlines that I've developed for workshops and training programs. They are meant both as ideas to help you design your own and as guides that you can lift directly from here to use as you see fit. These addenda do not have the same strict copyright obligations as the rest of the book, so feel free to use them as you need to. If you find a use for an outline or an exercise—use it. If you find a way to make one of the exercises better, or take pieces of one and add something else, do that. I would appreciate hearing about your efforts only because I want to be able to benefit from your experience and see how we can improve any of these exercises and outlines, create new ones, or delete those that aren't beneficial. It is only by working together that we're going to be able to stop rape.

## GROUP PROCESS: THE BASICS

Learning occurs on a number of levels: intellectual, emotional, and social. In order for learning to be effective, all of these levels must be utilized. Different people learn best in different ways. For some, a very cognitive process best encourages learning; for others, more emotive work utilizing guided imagery and group exercises works best; and for others a more social, interactive, discussion-oriented process best facilitates learning. Use whatever forms you are most comfortable using, but also be flexible and creative. Allow the participants as much leeway as you can throughout the time you're together.

Allow yourselves to learn and grow along with the participants. None of us, as men, have gotten so good at cleaning up our sexism, and challenging our rape-supporting attitudes and behavior, that we can't learn more. Facilitating a discussion successfully encourages dialogue.

Men traditionally learn and discuss issues in a very intellectual or cognitive manner that is very effective when learning numbers, facts, or logic. But it is also a way of keeping an emotional distance from difficult or sensitive issues. We are going to be discussing issues of sexual violence—issues which are, by definition, emotionally charged and very difficult. To most effectively learn requires we be in touch with our emotions. Stay aware of what you are feeling.

Whenever giving a presentation, you will probably have no more than two hours. As a result you will need to quickly assess the group. Look at its cohesiveness. Determine if it is a class that has been together for a couple of years, or whether it is a group of strangers who have only come together to attend the workshop. What's the age breakdown of the group? What are its racial, class, and gender divisions? Can you determine a natural leader in the group? Examine the ways that you can be effective with that group, given your particular style and comfort level. Try to convey a strong sense of mutuality (we're all in this together) as quickly as possible.

Begin by welcoming people and briefly describing the program of the day. Establish ground rules for the exercises and clarify expectations for the activities. Certain rules need to be explicitly stated from the beginning of the program:

- No violence will be tolerated during the activity. This includes verbal violence such as put-downs or oppressive comments.

- Participants must be reminded to respect themselves and each other. Additionally, assume that survivors are present, and make all comments with that in mind.

- Don't be judgmental of others' comments or remarks. Remember, we are learning together, and many of us are at different stages in our development.

- Agree not to use anything said during the discussion outside of the discussion or workshop.

○ Don't give advice to each other. Our purpose is to listen to each other and try and learn. Giving advice doesn't facilitate learning.

The purpose of any exercise is to stir up, and deal with, emotional material. By definition, this means that many of the participants are going to be feeling uncomfortable at times during the workshop. That is actually quite good. Allow and encourage participants and presenters permission to express their feelings. "Feeling good" is not the purpose of this activity—learning and growing is. However, participants may need to leave the room for a moment in order to regroup and as a means of taking care of themselves. We are coming together to discuss issues of sexual violence—a horrible issue. To *honestly* discuss and deal with issues of sexual violence means that you will not feel good.

# EXERCISES

## BRAINSTORMING "RAPE"

(10-20 minutes)
This is a very good ice-breaking exercise.

Have group members brainstorm and verbalize any and all words that come up in their minds when they hear the word "rape." It is important to emphasize that the words they come up with will not be identified with them, and that there isn't going to be any evaluating. List the words on a sheet of paper or chalkboard. Discuss the words that participants come up with and the emotional impact of each.

## CROSS-GENDER UNDERSTANDING

(20-30 minutes)
For mixed-gender workshops, this exercise is generally
good for people no younger than the high-school senior
level.

Ask all participants to describe in as much detail as they can how their lives would be different if they walked out of the workshop, or woke up the next morning, and there were no more rape.

Generally, the men will stumble towards an idea or two, and the women will get rolling with lists of ideas. The men frequently get floored at the intensity of the impact that rape and the threat of rape have on the lives of women. Encourage the men to notice what they are feeling, but to stay actively listening to what the women are saying.

Remind the men that these are the women in their lives: co-workers, mothers, friends, sisters, daughters, lovers. Also remind

159

them that most women are victimized by the men in their lives. If the women in men's lives were victimized by the men in their lives, then what's the relationship between the men sitting here in the room and the men who victimized their female friends?

## GUIDED IMAGERY

(30-45 minutes)
This was originally designed for men. However, it has been used with mixed-gender audiences, generally with good results.

Explain that they will be doing a guided imagery exercise and briefly describe what that entails. Explain that the exercise should take about twenty minutes and there will be time afterwards to process their feelings and thoughts. Ask how many of them have been involved in a guided imagery before. (If the number is low, allow extra time for relaxation.)

It is also important to assure the group that guided imagery techniques don't always work for everyone. If this process doesn't work for them, then the discussion should help in developing some new thoughts and feelings.

### Sample Guide

*Get as comfortable and as relaxed as possible. Uncross your arms and legs, and sit as comfortably as you can. Close your eyes and begin breathing deeply. In through you nose, out through your mouth. Begin with three deep breaths; with each, feel yourself becoming more and more a part of the chair you are sitting in. Feel the tension leave your body. Give yourself full permission to become completely relaxed and comfortable. With your mind's eye, imagine yourself sitting here in the room, on your chair, becoming more and more comfortable and relaxed. Imagine seeing the tension leaving your body with each breath. Notice the sounds in the room, including the sound of your breathing. Notice the temperature of the room—how does it feel? Simply enjoy the feeling of relaxation and comfort.*

*As you continue to relax, and breathe deeply, see yourself float to the top of the room. You now imagine yourself by the ceiling looking down at all of us. You see the chairs, the tops of our heads, the tops of the lights. Keep breathing deeply as you slip through the roof and are now outside [Facilitator Note—have your voice become a bit fainter]. You keep drifting upwards and notice the tops of cars, the tops of the buildings. Soon you are able to see the mountains and the ocean, and lakes. Slowly, you feel yourself floating back down onto a street in your neighborhood.*

*Imagine yourself walking down a city street. [Facilitator note—be specific about street name, location, and neighborhood.] Imagine that you are walking home from a restaurant after meeting some friends for dinner, and your mind is on the dinner and the conversation. It is well past dark, and you are walking to your car—alone. As you are walking, notice the temperature of the evening—is it warm? cool? is it humid? is the wind blowing? and so on. Notice the city noises that are going on around you, and the smells.*

*As you continue walking down the street, you notice a woman walking alone in front of you. She is walking towards you. You don't pay much more attention than to notice her presence, and you go back to thinking about the dinner. You continue walking, and once again, you notice her. You notice her appearing to nervously glance at you and then quickly look away. You notice that she has begun walking faster as the two of you draw nearer. You notice that her shoulders are raised up and curled inward—as if she is closing off to you. You attempt to draw her eye to connect with her and "be polite," and you notice that she seems to be avoiding your eye contact. In fact, she seems to be actively avoiding your eye contact.*

*Notice how you are feeling as you become aware that she is frightened of you. Notice what your heart is doing and the thoughts that come rushing up in your mind as you continue to consider that this woman is actually afraid of you. [Facilitator note—allow several moments for them to sit with the feelings and thoughts.] Now, you have passed each other, and these thoughts continue to swim through your brain. Suddenly you stop, as a second thought crashes into your thinking. You realize that you were walking alone as well, yet you felt no fear. You didn't feel threatened—certainly not as threatened as she appeared. You turn to look after her as you consider what it must be like to feel so threatened simply walking down the street. [Facilitator note—allow several moments for them to sit with these feelings and thoughts.]*

*I want you to continue an awareness of your thoughts and feelings as you slowly leave the street and reenter the room here. You become more and more aware that you are once again sitting in a chair, and that you are in a room with several other participants. You are aware, once again, of my voice. Begin noticing your breathing, and breathe in and out slowly three times—in through you nose, out through you mouth. When you are ready, open your eyes and bring yourself slowly back into the room.*

### Sample Process Narrative I

*I'd like for you to spend some time thinking about how the woman on the street may have felt. Think about what kinds of feelings she may have been having—what kinds of thoughts may have been going through her head. Try and put yourself, if you can, in her shoes and consider what that experience may have been like for her. Remember that she has grown up in a culture where she has been taught to expect to be raped.*

Here is a typical list of descriptive words that frequently come up: frightened, confused, nervous, powerless, alone, angry, distrusting, vulnerable.

*Note that many of the feelings and thoughts raised during this part of the exercise are very similar to the feelings and thoughts labeled by women who have been victimized by sexual violence. [Facilitator Note—allow ample time for processing these feelings and thoughts.]*

### Sample Process Narrative II

*Now I'd like for you to talk a bit about what you felt and thought during the imagery and afterward. What are you thinking and feeling right now? What were your different feelings and thoughts during the imagery itself? I'm going to go ahead and list the emotions, thoughts, and main themes that we come up with.*

Here is a typical list of brainstormed words: frustrated, discouraged, defensive, blamed, guilty, ashamed, disappointed, angry, confused, upset, "like I want to yell, 'I'm not going to do anything to hurt you!'", sad.

Encourage the participants to come up with the descriptive terms, since that tends to be much more useful for the participants.

## TYPICAL MEN AND TYPICAL WOMEN

(15 minutes)

Divide the chalkboard or writing space into two columns. On one side, have the participants list the "typical" characteristics of men as are displayed in the world (through the media and culture). On the other side, ask the participants to list the "typical" characteristics of women. Lead a discussion about what this demonstrates. "Who would you rather be if you were on a street at night? Who would you hire for a manager's position? Who would you rather have for a secretary or in a support-level job? Who would you rather go to after a tragedy to grieve?"

## THE CONTINUUM OF OUR VALUES

(20 minutes)

Have the participants stand up. Explain to them that they will be participating in an interactive exercise which will place them, physically, along a continuum. There are no "right" or "wrong" answers in this exercise. Rather, this is an opportunity for them to better identify their own belief systems, and to offer an opportunity for those belief systems to be challenged. Explain that they will be asked to defend their decision to stand where they choose, but they also have the right to refuse to explain their stance.

Describe a continuum along the floor. With each of the statements—which are all set up as yes/no statements, ask the participants to take a physical position along the continuum which most demonstrates how much they agree with, disagree with, or are neutral to each statement. Then ask them to explain why they picked that position to stand.

Sample statements:
- Prostitutes can't be raped.
- Some women lie about being raped.
- What a person wears could suggest their desire for sex.
- Women shouldn't go to a bar alone.

## WHEN HAVE YOU FELT VULNERABLE?

(20 minutes)

Break down into small groups of three to five members each. Ask that the members in the group discuss with each other times when they have felt vulnerable and frightened. Decide on a reporter who will take notes from what is said in the small group.

Say something like, "Discuss situations when you felt vulnerable and unsafe. During those times, examine how you may have felt forced. When you felt forced to do something you did not want to do, what was that like?" Allow them several moments to discuss within the small groups. After a period of time, have them come back to the larger group to discuss what they talked about in the smaller groups. Spend several moments processing with them about the memories, and the exercise itself.

## DISCLOSING

(20-30 minutes)

This is a good ice-breaking exercise which can be used at any time during the activity.

Have the participants divide into pairs picking someone they do not know very well. Ask them to disclose to their partner a personal secret. After a couple of minutes, ask them to reverse roles and the other person discloses a secret of theirs. (People will only share what they are comfortable with sharing and will go no further.) The person listening should not push for more information. Have them come back into the larger group and discuss what that process was like for them—both as the listening and disclosing. No details should be shared with the larger group.

## PROCESSING

(20-30 minutes)
This is a good exercise to use repeatedly throughout the
activity, especially after more-intense discussions.

Have the group participants break into small groups of three to five members each. Allow them time to process the information they just learned. Offer an opportunity to label and express the feelings that came up for them. Reinforce that there are likely survivors in the room with memories and pain stirred up during the discussion. Acknowledge participants' right to leave for personal reasons—no questions will be asked or allowed (except to see if someone needs to be alone or wants to talk). Return to the larger group and see if there are any people willing to share what went on in the smaller groups without identifying anyone.

## DECISION MAKING

(5-10 minutes)
Hand out small pieces of paper and pens or pencils. Ask the participants to write down the last five decisions that they remember making. Do not offer a time frame within which these decisions may have been made. Allow about five minutes for them to write down their thoughts.

During the discussion phase of this exercise, attempt to raise the awareness of their *deciding* to answer the questions, or write those answers down, or come to the workshop, or even listen to you as the presenter. All of those are choices that participants have made, but may not be consciously recognized as choices.

## WORKING WITH THE MEDIA

(15 minutes)
Break off into pairs. Have one partner play the role of a media person, and the other the role of a representative of an event. Have the "media person" ask a variety of questions that are in some way related to issues of sexual violence. The responsibility of the "event spokesperson" is to answer the questions in only one sentence.

To assist in the process, have a handful of questions prepared for the media person to ask. Some questions could include: "Why are men coming together to speak out on rape?" "What is the point of your being here?" and "Why are you here?"

# SAMPLE PRESENTATION OUTLINES

Before any presentation, always acknowledge that there are likely to be survivors in the room. Encourage survivors to do what they need to during the discussion to feel safe. Also ensure that others in the room take the presentation and discussion seriously.

*Men's Responsibility (1-1 1/2 hour workshop)*

    I. Introduction
           of the presenter(s)
           of the topic and terms
                survivor
                victim
                empowerment
                etc.
   II. Definitions
           define rape
           rape behaviors
           the rape continuum
                the connections between rape and other forms of sexism
                    and sexist behavior
  III. Benefits
           discuss the benefits men receive as a result of rape
           examine benefits for men working to dismantle male
                supremacy
  IV. Guilt vs. Responsibility
   V.  How to take Responsibility/What to do
  VI. Conclusion

Sections IV and V should be the longest sections of the presentation.

*Men Responding to Survivors   (1-1 1/2 hour workshop)*

    I. Introduction
        of the presenter(s)
        of the topics and terms
    II. Responses to Rape
        Rape Trauma Syndrome
        what the survivor may be going through
    III. Men's Responses to Rape
        emotional responses
        behavioral responses
    IV. What men can do to be supportive
        offer a full discussion opportunity for men responding to
            survivor issues
    V. Conclusion

*Rape and Racism (2 hour workshop)*

    I.Introduction of Terms
        what is rape
        what is racism
    II. How Rape Affects People's Lives
        personal trauma
        politics of rape
    III. The Effects of Racism
        on individuals
        on the culture
    IV.The Myth (Lie) of the Man of Color Rapist
        most rapes are intraracial
        those rapes that are interracial tend to have white men
            raping women and men of color
    V. Extra Risks that Women of Color Face
        victimized by men of color and white men
        less frequently believed when reporting
    VI. Ways that White Male Culture Has Used Both Rape and Racism
        to continue the oppression of both women and people
            of color

*Male Survivors (2 hours)*

    I. Introduction to Rape
        definitions
        rape as a violent act
        why rape is so devastating to victim/survivors
    II.Male Rape
        difference between "homosexual rape" and male rape
        most men are raped by heterosexual men
            rape during gay-bashing attacks
            sexual assault as process of male bonding
                in prison
                in fraternities
                in military
        men more likely to be victimized by groups and to have
        weapons used
   III. Men's Response to Being Raped
        very similar to women's response
        heightened issues:
            homophobia—question own sexuality
            AIDS
            issues of anger and power
   IV. Politics of Male Rape
        rape is used as a way of maintaining the social
            order—white and male supremacy
                history of sexual assault during lynchings
                heterosexual men bashing and sexually assaulting
                    gay men and lesbians
                rape in prison
        rape of men is kept quiet to reinforce the notion that "rape
        is supposed to happen to women, not to men" thereby
        strengthening the attitudes that encourage the rape
        of women

*Men and Pornography*

    I. What is Pornography?
        two-dimensional
        male fantasies of women, men, and sex
        noninteractive
        noncommunicative
        all physical sensation with no feelings attached
    II. Pornography as Violence
        how pornography reinforces rape attitudes
            depicts sexual dehumanizing behaviors as erotic
            depicts women as two-dimensional
            depicts women as enjoying humiliation
        pornography, in and of itself, as violence
            buying human being is violence
            pornography as man-made image of woman
   III. Pornography and Sex
        men's first sexual experiences tend to be with pornography
        how this experiences may influence men's later experiences
            with sex

# CONTACT LIST

The following organizations are good resources for more information on the topics discussed in this book.

National Coalition Against Sexual Assault (NCASA)
Cassandra Thomas, President
c/o Houston Area Women's Center Rape Crisis Program
3101 Richmond Ave., Suite 150
Washington, DC 77098
(713) 528-6798

Men's Anti-Rape Resource Center
P.O. Box 73559
Washington, DC 20056
(202) 529-7239

Ending Men's Violence Network
Craig Norberg-Bohm, Coordinator
50 Wyman St.
Arlington, MA 02174
(617) 648-5957

Activist Men's Journal
c/o Geov Parrish
P.O. Box 85541
Seattle, WA 98145

Young Women's Project
Nadia Moritz, E.D.
Suite 428
1511 K St., N.W.
Washington, DC 20005
(202) 393-0461

National Clearinghouse on Marital and Date Rape
Laura X, Ed.D.
Women's History Research Center
2325 Oak St.
Berkeley, CA 94708
(510) 524-1582

Clearinghouse on Femicide
P.O. Box 12342
Berkeley, CA 94701-3342
(510) 845-7005

National Black Women's Health Project
Cynthia Newbille
1237 Gordon St., S.W.
Atlanta, GA 30310
(404) 758-9590

Women Hurt in Systems of Prostitution Engaged in Revolt
(WHISPER)
P.O. Box 8719
Lake Street Station
Minneapolis, MN 55408
(612) 644-6301

# BIBLIOGRAPHY

## RAPE

Barry, Kathleen. *Female Sexual Slavery*. New York: New York University Press, 1979.

Brownmiller, Susan. *Against Our Will: Men, Women and Rape*. New York: Bantam Books,1975.

Connell, Noreen, and Wilson, Cassandra. *Rape: The First Sourcebook for Women*. (New York Radical Feminists). New York: New American Library, 1974.

Estrich, Susan. *Real Rape: How the Legal System Victimizes Women Who Say No*. Cambridge, Mass.: Harvard University Press,1987.

Finkelhor, David, and Kersti Yllo. *License to Rape: Sexual Abuse of Wives*. New York: The Free Press, 1985.

Gager, Nancy, and Cathleen Schurr. *Sexual Assault: Confronting Rape in America*. New York: Grosset and Dunlap, 1976.

Gordon, Margaret T., and Stephanie Riger. *The Female Fear*. New York: The Free Press,1989.

Kelly, Liz. *Surviving Sexual Violence*. Minneapolis: University of Minnesota Press, 1988.

Russell, Diana E. H. *The Politics of Rape: The Victim's Perspective*. New York: Scarborough House, 1974.

————. *Rape in Marriage*. Bloomington, In.: Indiana University Press, 1982.

————. *Sexual Exploitation: Rape, Child Sexual Abuse, and Workplace Harrassment*. Newbury Park, Calif.: Sage, 1984.

————. *The Secret Trauma: Incest in the Lives of Girls and Women*. New York: Basic Books, 1986.

Sanday, Peggy Reeves. *Gang Rape: Sex, Brotherhood, and Privilege on Campus*. New York: New York University Press, 1990.

Scully, Diane. *Understanding Sexual Violence: A Study of Convicted Rapists*. Cambridge, Mass.: Unwin Hyman, 1990.
Warshaw, Robin. *I Never Called it Rape*. New York: Harper & Row, 1988.

## SEXUAL HARASSMENT

Alliance Against Sexual Coercion. *Fighting Sexual Harassment*. Boston: Alyson Publications,1981.
Black Scholar, ed. *Court of Appeal: The Black Community Speaks Out on the Racial and Sexual Politics of Thomas vs. Hill*. New York: Ballantine Books, 1992.
Dziech, Billie Wright, and Linda Weiner.*The Lecherous Professor: Sexual Harassment on Campus*. Urbana, Il.: University of Illinois Press,1990.
MacKinnon, Catherine A. *Sexual Harassment of Working Women*. New Haven, Conn.: Yale University Press, 1979.
Morrison, Toni, ed. *Race-ing Justice, En-gendering Power: Essays on Anita Hill, Clarence Thomas, and the Construction of Social Reality*. New York: Pantheon Books,1992.
Paludi, Michelle A., ed. *Ivory Power: Sexual Harassment on Campus*. Albany, N.Y.: State University of New York Press,1990.
Pendergrass, Virginia E., ed. *Women Winning: A Handbook for Action Against Sex Discrimination*. Chicago: Nelson Hall Publishers,1979.

## PORNOGRAPHY

Dworkin, Andrea, and Catherinen MacKinnon. *Pornography and Civil Rights: A New Day for Women's Equality*. Available from Southern Sisters, Inc., 411 Morris St., Durham, N.C. 27701,1988.
Griffin, Susan. *Pornography and Silence: Culture's Revenge Against Nature*. New York: Harper & Row,1981.
Gubar, Susan, and Joan Hoff. *For Adult Users Only: The Dilemma of Violent Pornography*. Bloomington, In.: Indiana University Press,1989.
Kappelar, Suzanne. *The Pornography of Representation*. Minneapolis: University of Minnesota Press,1986.
Leidholdt, Dorchen, and Janice G. Raymond. *The Sexual Liberals and the Attack on Feminism*. New York: Pergamon Press, 1990.
Lerderer, Laura. *Take Back the Night: Women on Pornography*. New York: William Morrow, 1980.

## BATTERING AND DATING VIOLENCE

Levy, Barrie, ed. *Dating Violence: Young Women in Danger*. Seattle: The Seal Press, 1991.

McShane, Claudette. *Warning! Dating May be Hazardous to Your Health*. Racine, Wis.: Mother Courage Press, 1988.

NiCarthy, Ginn. *Getting Free: A Handbook for Women in Abusive Relationships*. Seattle: The Seal Press, 1982.

———. *The Ones Who Got Away: Women Who Left Abusive Partners*. Seattle: The Seal Press, 1987.

Schecter, Susan. *Women and Male Violence: The Visions and Struggles of the Battered Women's Movement*. Boston: South End Press, 1982.

Stanko, Elizabeth A. *Intimate Intrusions: Women's Experience of Male Violence*. New York: Routledge Press, 1985.

## WOMEN'S LIBERATION/ THEORY OF MEN'S VIOLENCE

Cameron, Deborah and Elizabeth Frazer. *The Lust to Kill: A Feminist Investigation of Sexual Murder*. New York: New York University Press, 1987.

Caputi, Jane. *The Age of Sex Crime*. Bowling Green, Ohio: Bowling Green State University Press, 1987.

Dworkin, Andrea. *Women Hating*. New York: E. P. Dutton, 1974.

———. *Our Blood: Prophecies and Discourses on Sexual Politics*. New York: G.P. Putnam & Sons, 1976.

———. *Pornography: Men Possessing Women*. New York: G. P. Putnam & Sons, 1981.

———. *Right Wing Women*, New York: G. P. Putnam & Sons, 1983.

———. *Letters From a War Zone*. New York: E. P. Dutton, 1988.

French, Marilyn. *Beyond Power: On Women, Men and Morals*. New York: Ballantine Books, 1985.

Hanmer, Jalna, Jill Radford, and Elizabeth Stanko, eds. *Women, Policing, and Male Violence: International Perspectives*. New York: Routledge, 1989.

Janseen-Jurreit, Marielouise. *Sexism: The Male Monopoly on History and Thought*. New York: Farrar, Straus, & Giroux, 1982.

Kaye/Kantrowitz, Melanie. *The Issue is Power: Essays on Women, Jews, Violence and Resistance*. San Francisco: Aunt Lute Foundation Books, 1992.

Malette, Louise and Marie Chalouh, eds. *The Montreal Massacre*. Charlottetown, Price Edward Island: Gynergy Books, 1991.

Morgan, Robin. *Sisterhood is Powerful*. New York: Vintage Books, 1970.

———. *Going Too Far: A Personal Account of a Feminist*. New York: Random House, 1968.

————. *The Anatomy of Freedom: Feminism, Physics, and Global Politics.* New York: Doubleday Anchor,1984.

————. *The Demon Lover: On The Sexuality of Terrorism.* New York: W. W. Norton, 1989.

Sanday, Peggy Reeves. *Female Power and Male Dominance: On the Origins of Sexual Inequality.* New York: Press Syndicate, 1981.

Schaef, Anne Wilson. *Women's Reality: An Emerging Female System in a White Male Society.* Minneapolis: Winston Press, 1981.

## FIGHTING BACK

Delacoste, Frederique and Felice Newman, eds. *Fight Back!: Feminist Resistance to Male Violence.* Minneapolis: Cleis Press, 1981.

## FEMINISM AND NONVIOLENCE

Coover, Virginia, Ellen Deacon, Charles Esser, and Christopher Moore, eds. *Resource Manual for a Living Revolution: A Handbook of Skills and Tools for Social Change Activists.* Philadelphia: New Society Publishers, 1985.

Davies, Miranda, ed. *Third World/Second Sex: Women's Struggles and National Liberation.* London: Zed Books, 1983.

Deming, Barbara. *Remembering Who We Are.* Tallahassee, Fla.: Pagoda Publications,1981.

Freire, Paulo. *Pedagogy of the Oppressed.* New York: Continuum Publishing Co.,1990.

McAllister, Pam, ed. *Reweaving the Web of Life: Feminism and Nonviolence.* Philadelphia: New Society Publishers, 1982.

————. *You Can't Kill the Spirit.* Philadelphia: New Society Publishers, 1988.

————. *The River of Courage: Generations of Women's Actions and Resistance.* Philadelphia: New Society Publishers, 1991.

Meyerding, Jane, ed. *We Are all Part of One Another: A Barbara Deming Reader.* Philadelphia: New Society Publishers, 1984.

## WOMEN OF COLOR

Anzaldúa, Gloria, ed. *Making Face, Making Soul: Creative and Critical Perspectives by Women of Color.* San Francisco: Aunt Lute Foundation, 1990.

Anzaldúa, Gloria and Cherríe Moraga, eds. *This Bridge Called My Back: Writings by Radical Women of Color.* New York: Kitchen Table Press, 1981.

Asian Women United of California. *Making Waves: An Anthology of Writings by and about Asian American Women.* Boston: Beacon Press, 1989.

Davis, Angela. *Women, Race, and Class.* New York: Random House, 1983.

Giddings, Paula. *When and Where I Enter: The Impact of Black Women on Race and Sex in America.* New York: Bantam, 1985.

hooks, bell. *Ain't I A Woman: Black Women and Feminism.* Boston: South End Press, 1981.

———. *Talking Back: Thinking Feminist, Thinking Black.* Boston: South End Press, 1989.

———. *Yearning: Race, Gender, and Cultural Politics.* Boston: South End Press, 1990.

———. *Black Looks: Race and Representation.* Boston: South End Press, 1992

Jaimes, M. Annette. *The State of Native America: Genocide, Colonization and Resistance.* Boston: South End, 1992.

King, Victoria. *Manhandled: Black Females, Breaking the Bondage and Reclaiming our Lives.* Nashville: Winston-Derek Publishers, 1992.

Lerner, Genda. *Black Woman in White America.* New York: Vintage Books, 1973.

## LESBIAN AND GAY LIBERATION

Comstock, Gary David. *Violence Against Lesbians and Gay Men.* New York: Columbia University Press, 1991.

Herek, Gegory M. and Kevin T. Berrill. *Hate Crimes: Confronting Violence Against Lesbians and Gay Men.* Newbury Park, Calif.: Sage Publications, 1992.

Pharr, Suzanne. *Homophobia: A Weapon of Sexism.* Inverness, Calif.: Chardon Press, 1988.

## MEN

Beneke, Timothy. *Men on Rape: What They Have to Say about Sexual Violence.* New York: St. Martin's Press,1982.

Chesler, Phyllis. *About Men.* New York: Bantam Books, 1978.

Ehrenreich, Barbara. *The Hearts of Men: American Dreams and the Flight from Commitment.* New York: Doubleday Anchor, 1983.

Kimmel, Michael S. *Changing Men: New Direction in Research on Men and Masculinity.* Newbury Park, Calif.: Sage Publications, 1987.

————, ed. *Men Confront Pornography*. New York: Crown Publishers,1990.

Kivel, Paul. *Men's Work: How to Stop the Violence that Tears Our Lives Apart*. New York: Ballantine Books, 1992.

McMullen, Richie J. *Male Rape: Breaking the Silence on the Last Taboo*. Boston: Alyson Publications, 1990.

Stoltenberg, John. *Refusing to Be a Man: Essays on Sex and Justice*. New York: Meridian Books,1989.

————. *The End of Manhood: A Book for Men of Consciousness*. New York: Dutton, 1993.

Snodgrass, Jon, ed. *For Men Against Sexism*. Albion, Calif.: Time Change Press, 1977.

Wooden, Wayne S. and Jay Parker. *Men Behind Bars: Sexual Exploitation in Prison*. New York: De Capo Press,1983.

## CHILDREN

Goldstein, Joseph, Anna Freud, and Albert J. Solnit. *Beyond the Best Interests of the Child*. New York: MacMillian, 1973.

Gross, Beatrice and Ronald Gross. *The Children's Right Movement: Overcoming the Oppression of Young People*. New York: Doubleday Anchor, 1977.

Miller, Alice. *Thou Shalt Not Be Aware: Society's Betrayal of the Child*. New York: New American Library, 1984.